While there is really no substitute for a good teacher, the beginner will find that with this book he can go a long way in teaching himself to play the violin. The instrument itself is first described and basic musical theory introduced. The functions of the two hands and how to develop their technique are then discussed, together with further points of theory that the violinist should know about. Later chapters cover sight-reading and memorising, phrasing, style and interpretation, playing with others, the history of the violin, and making minor repairs to the instrument. A guide to violin music is also included, and suggestions for pieces and studies to practice and books for further study are given throughout.

TEACH YOURSELF BOOKS

THE VIOLIN

Theodore Rowland-Entwistle

TEACH YOURSELF BOOKS
Hodder and Stoughton

First printed 1967
Fourth impression 1976

Copyright © 1967
Hodder and Stoughton Ltd

ISBN 0 340 05992 3

Printed in Great Britain
for Hodder & Stoughton Paperbacks,
a division of Hodder & Stoughton Ltd.,
Mill Road, Dunton Green, Sevenoaks, Kent
by Richard Clay (The Chaucer Press), Ltd., Bungay, Suffolk

Contents

Acknowledgements

The author would like to thank Mr. John Howard-Lucy and Mr. Stuart Wynn-Jones for much valuable advice; Mr. Alfred Crossberg for his careful work on the photographs; Miss Elaine Burrows for the loan of many specialist books; and especially Miss Jean Cooke for her encouragement, criticism, and help in the final preparation of the manuscript.

He would also like to acknowledge his gratitude to Mr. Hullah Brown for teaching him how to make music on the violin.

For Jean

1. Introduction

The first question you will probably ask is "Can you teach yourself to play the violin?" The answer is yes. If you wish to become a brilliant virtuoso there is no substitute for good lessons and hard practice, but you can go a long way in teaching yourself. In a sense, even the greatest virtuosos teach themselves. It is how they themselves work at and understand what they are taught that counts in the long run. Much of their advanced technique is entirely self-taught.

This book is designed to help the following people: first, those who know nothing of the violin, cannot have lessons, but want to learn; second, those who have had some lessons, perhaps many years before, and want to take up the instrument again; and third, those who are able to have some lessons, but need more help than their teachers can give them. In this third class belong many children who have lessons at school, sometimes in classes with insufficient personal attention, sometimes from teachers for whom the violin is a second instrument. It is possible to get a great way on one's own, or with the minimum of help. My first few years of violin-playing were self-taught, and I later studied with a very great teacher who was himself largely self-taught. In these days there are many more visual and aural aids to learning. Make the fullest possible use of radio, television, records, and tape-recorders. Watch, and listen to, good players as much as possible. Television programmes often include excellent close-ups of great players in action, and you can study their technique at close hand and relate it to what you yourself are doing. The more you listen to broadcast music and records, the more you will learn what the sound ought to be like—and that is of enormous help in achieving the desired result. If you have a tape-recorder you can record your own playing and listen to it critically. A word of warning: a tape-recorder seems to accentuate all one's worst faults. This is a good thing, but do not let yourself be discouraged by the sounds you hear. They sound much worse recorded than live, though nothing will disguise playing out of tune.

You should use this book in conjunction with an ordinary violin tutor, method, or course. These books are designed for use by a teacher; consequently they have all the exercises and examples you need, but remarkably little in the way of explanation. This book is designed to provide the additional information a teacher would give. Because the two hands of a violinist have to perform different functions, it is necessary to study the work of the two hands separately but simultaneously. Accordingly, you should regard Chapters 7 and 9 as being concurrent, and also study the chapters on musical theory at the same time. Progress is a matter of regular and careful work, and an ability to make haste slowly.

Remember that your purpose in learning the violin is to enjoy it. Try to find others who play, and play with them. Here, let me give a further word of warning: before you imitate other players, or take their advice, listen to their own playing. If it is good, it is probably safe to follow them. If it is not good, don't imitate them.

Before you begin, you will need material to play and study, including exercises, scales, studies and pieces. Any of the following are good, but you could choose other equivalent books from the many available.

Tutors and Exercises

The Hullah Brown–Spencer Dyke Violin Method. Joseph Williams. This is designed for adult learners as well as younger players.

Ottakar Ševčík Violin Method. Bosworth and Co.

Preliminary Exercises, by Adam Carse. Augener.

Studies

First Graded Studies for the Violin, edited by Sidney Rob-
    johns. Bosworth.
Progressive Studies, edited by Spencer Dyke. Joseph
    Williams. Graded: the first and second grades are suitable
    for beginners.

Scales

The Spencer Dyke Scale Book. Joseph Williams.

Pieces

Hours of Pleasure, Book 1, by Adam Carse. Augener.
    Further information on pieces and studies is given in
Chapters 12 and 15.

2. How a Violin Works

The violin is one of the most expressive and flexible musical instruments. Like the human voice, it can produce notes loud or soft, swelling or dying away, rich and sonorous or bright and clear. Because of this almost human quality, a great deal of mystery surrounds the violin. Probably many players are puzzled as to how it works, in the same way that many drivers do not understand how the mechanism of a car works. But just as a driver will handle a car better if he understands what is happening under the bonnet, so a player will get better results from his instrument if he knows exactly why what he is doing produces the results that he hears.

Beginners may prefer to read this chapter through quickly, just to gain a general idea of its content. More advanced players should study it carefully, so that they can relate what they are learning to the "mechanics" of the violin. They are less likely to make unpleasant sounds if they know what it is they do that produces these sounds, and why.

How the Violin is Made

If you stretch a rubber band between two fingers and pluck it, it gives out a faint note. If you stretch the band across the open top of a wooden box and then pluck it, you get a much louder sound. The box amplifies the sound of the rubber band. Basically, the body of a violin is a wooden box which amplifies the sound of the four strings that are stretched across it. The violin is a special kind of box, made of carefully chosen wood and designed to get the best possible amplification of the sound of its strings.

See Plate 1 for the parts of the violin. The body of a violin is about 14 inches long. The top plate, or belly, is the real sounding-board of the instrument. It is made from a piece of soft, straight-grained pine cut on the quarter: that is, the wood has been cut like a slice of cake, and not just sawn straight across the log. The wedge-shaped piece of wood is cut in two again, and the resulting two smaller wedges are joined at their thick ends to form a single piece shaped like a shallow roof. The belly is then carved out of the solid piece. It is not bent to shape in any way. Round the edge three thin pieces of inlay, known as purfling, are let in to help stop the wood from splitting, and also as decoration. The *f*-holes allow the sound to escape from the body of the violin. The nicks in the *f*-holes mark the position of the bridge.

The back of the violin is made of a hard wood, generally maple or sycamore, cut and carved in the same way as the front. Sometimes a back is made in one piece from a plank sawn straight across the log. This kind of back is known as a slab back. The ribs of the violin, which are the part between the back and the belly, are made of curly-grained maple, match-box thin, heated and bent to shape. Blocks of wood inside the violin help to strengthen it. The parts of the violin are put together with hot glue. No screws or nails are used. The neck of the violin and the head, where the pegs are, are usually made of maple or sycamore. The pegs, on which the strings are wound, are a friction-tight fit, carefully adjusted so that they can be turned readily but will not slip. The finger-board, which has to take a lot of hard wear, and the tail-piece, which holds the strings at the other end, are made of ebony. So is the nut, the little bar of wood over which the strings run as they leave the peg-box.

There are three other important parts of a violin. The bridge, made of maple, supports the strings, and conducts their vibrations to the body of the violin. The sound-post, made of pine, is fitted between the back and the belly inside the violin. It helps to support the belly against the pressure of the strings (which is more than 20 lb.), and conducts the vibrations of the strings from the belly to the back. The exact position of the bridge and the sound-post can alter the tone of a violin enormously, and so that they can be adjusted readily, neither is glued into place. The third important part of the instrument is the bass-bar, a strip of pine which is glued under the belly on the left side of the violin as the player looks at it. It comes under the lower, or bass, strings of the instrument—hence the name. The bass-bar helps to strengthen the violin, and also alters the way in which the belly vibrates. The violin has four strings, which are made of gut, metal, or gut and metal.

The difference between a good violin and a bad one lies largely in the way it has been made. A craftsman making a violin by hand chooses the wood of the various parts with care, so that the tone qualities of the woods will blend. He shapes the parts with equal care, and finally uses a good varnish which will protect the wood without having too great a damping effect on its vibrations. The very cheapest fiddles are cut and shaped largely by machinery. Many low-priced violins, including many of considerable age, are mass-produced by hand on a sort of conveyor-belt system. One man makes nothing but backs, say, and another nothing but necks and scrolls, while yet another specialises in assembling the parts into complete fiddles. It is thus a matter of luck whether the parts are really well-matched, although each may be individually well made. Sometimes the parts do match perfectly, and the result is a cheap fiddle with a superb tone. But such instruments are rare. The difference between a good violin and a bad one is similar to that between a piece of precision machinery, in which every part is individually made and fitted by hand, and a mass-produced car built on an assembly line.

How the Bow is Made

The stick of a bow is made of a springy wood called Pernambuco wood, which comes from Brazil. The stick is carved to shape from a solid piece of wood, and the curve is put in by heating the stick and bending it to shape. At one end is a sliding part, called the frog or nut, to which one end of the hair is attached. The frog is made of ebony, often decorated with silver and mother-of-pearl. A screw thread set in the end of the stick moves the nut to and fro, and enables the player to tighten the hair against the spring of the stick. The other end of the hair is attached to the head of the bow, which is carved in one piece with the stick. The hair comes from the tails of white horses, and there are between 150 and 200 hairs on a bow. The surface of each hair is covered with tiny 'teeth' that grip the string as the bow is drawn across it and, like the violin strings, the hair wears out and has to be replaced from time to time.

How the Sound is Produced

If you pluck the lowest string of a violin, you can see the string vibrate. This movement of the string moves the air around it, and sets up sound-waves which reach our ears, so that we hear the note. But as we saw with the experiment with the rubber band, the vibration of a string by itself does not move the air very much. It needs an amplifier—the violin. The body of the violin vibrates in sympathy with the string, and produces a much larger movement of air, and therefore a much louder note.

After you pluck a string, the sound soon dies away. To produce a constant note, the player needs a method of plucking the string repeatedly and very fast. That is exactly what the hair of the bow does. The violinist rubs rosin on the hair to make it rough. As the roughened hair moves across the string, it gives the string a rapid succession of tugs, which cause the string to vibrate constantly. In between each tug, the hair lets go of the string so that it can vibrate. If you pass a perfectly smooth object, such as a knitting-needle, over the string you will get hardly any noise. The knitting-needle is not tugging the string sufficiently, and is remaining in contact with it so that the vibrations are checked.

The Work of the Left Hand

The pitch of a note given out by a string depends largely on its length, together with its thickness and its tension. The longer the string, the deeper the note. Thicker and less tensely stretched strings produce deeper notes than thin, taut ones.

The violin's four strings all have the same effective length. They vary in thickness and tension, so they produce four different notes. To produce other notes, the player must temporarily shorten the strings. He does this by putting the tips of his fingers firmly on the strings, pressing them into contact with the finger-board. The farther up the finger-board he presses the strings down, the shorter the strings become and the higher the notes. There are seven basic positions for the hand as it moves up the finger-board towards the bridge. The first position is with the hand at its farthest distance away from the bridge.

The Work of the Right Hand

The right hand guides the bow across the string so as to make the string vibrate in the way that the player wants. The player can vary the tone he produces by a combination of three things: the speed with which he passes the bow across the string; the pressure with which he forces the bow against the string; and the point on the string at which the bow makes contact. A vibrating string vibrates not only as a whole, but in parts as well. The presence of the bow on the string damps or checks some vibrations, and the point on the string at which it makes contact determines which vibrations are checked. The player can also pluck the strings with his fingers.

Variations of Tone

The tone of the four strings of a violin varies, and composers and players make good use of this variation to add to the special effects that can be obtained on the violin. By using the higher positions of the left hand, the same note can often be played on more than one string. Higher notes played on the lower strings have a rich, sonorous quality, in contrast to the brightness the notes have when played on the higher strings. A very good example of the use of this tone quality is the *Air on the G String*, the arrangement which the German violinist August Wilhelmj made of a movement from J. S. Bach's Suite in D Major for orchestra. The notes of this piece could be played using three of the four strings. But Wilhelmj directs them to be played entirely on the fourth, or G, string, because of the rich tone of that string.

Harmonics are another special effect. If you halve the length of a string, it will give the same note but an octave higher (for an explanation of *octave* and similar musical terms see Chapter 6). If you touch the string lightly at the middle point, both halves of the string will vibrate when it is bowed, giving a clear, bell-like note called a harmonic. A number of other harmonics can be produced by similarly touching the string at certain points so that it vibrates in other equal parts, such as quarters, fifths, and so on. The points at which the string is touched to produce harmonics are called nodes, or nodal points. Artificial harmonics are produced by stopping the string with one finger, thus shortening the string, and touching it lightly with another finger to sound a harmonic on the shortened string.

Another type of tone is known as *con sordino*, two Italian words meaning *with the mute*. It is a thin, veiled tone, with little resonance. A mute is a small clip that fits on to the bridge, and stiffens it. The holes in the bridge are not only for decoration; they divide the bridge in effect into four bridges, so that each of the four strings can vibrate separately. The mute in effect makes the bridge solid. The result is that when one string is vibrating and making the bridge vibrate, the other strings act as check-ropes and damp the vibrations of the bridge, rather in the way that the guy-ropes of a tent prevent it from moving in the breeze.

3. The Equipment

A violin student needs a violin, a chin-rest and a shoulder-rest to enable him to hold it, a bow, rosin, a mute, a tuning fork, a case to contain all these items, and a stand to support his music. This sounds a formidable list, but in fact it is not. The violin is one of the cheapest instruments for the beginner. He can start playing for less than a would-be wind-instrument player, and the cost of the cheapest piano in good working order is usually much more than a comparable correctly-fitted violin with a reasonable bow.

The Instrument

The violin you choose will depend on the amount you are prepared to spend, and your personal knowledge and preference. It is possible to obtain a complete outfit—violin, bow and case—for about £5. If you can afford no more to begin with, then buy such an outfit. As you make progress you will want something better, and you should then endeavour to obtain a better instrument. But you can learn the rudiments of fingering and bowing just as well on a cheap fiddle as on a Stradivarius.

Good violins, like good wine, improve with age. Ideally, for your first instrument you should try to find an old violin in good condition, probably in the price range of £15 to £20. If possible, ask someone who plays to help you to choose an instrument, and to try it for you. It would be desirable to buy your first instrument from a violin dealer, or from a reputable music shop. Violins bought in antique or general second-hand shops are always a gamble. This is because two things are of the utmost importance in a fiddle: condition and correct fitting-up.

Your violin must not be unglued at any point, nor should it have any serious open cracks in it. Most violins of any age have a few cracks, but these should have been properly repaired. To test that the violin is properly glued up, tap gently with a finger knuckle all the way round the edge of the back and belly. If anything is loose you will hear a distinct rattle. Beware of cracks in the back, and particularly cracks that run under the foot of the sound-post. A bad crack under the sound-post is almost impossible to repair well. Check that the pegs turn readily, but do not slip when they have been turned. The finger-board should not be worn. If it is grooved or pitted where the fingers have pressed the strings into it, you will find the instrument difficult, if not impossible, to play in tune. The bridge of the instrument should be straight and not bent in any way.

As for the fitting up, it would need a practised eye to see whether this had been correctly done. But there are some points you can watch out for. The feet of the bridge should sit firmly on the belly of the violin, with no gaps showing. The bridge should lean very slightly away from the finger-board. The notches in the top should be evenly spaced, and not too deep. The bridge should be slightly higher on the left side—from the player's viewpoint—than on the other. This slight increase in height raises the string that is farthest away from the bow arm, and makes it easier to reach with the bow. The strings should not be too high above the finger-board—the thickness of a postcard at the nut, and ranging from $\frac{3}{16}$ in. to $\frac{1}{4}$ in. at the end of the finger-board. If they are higher, they will be difficult to press down; if lower, they may tend to rattle on the finger-board when they are vibrating.

Chin-rests and shoulder-rests are necessary so that you can hold the violin with your chin, entirely without the left hand. The chin-rest is clamped permanently on the violin. It keeps the player's chin off the body of the fiddle, and gives it a ridge to grip on. The height and pattern of the chin-rest must be chosen to suit the individual player. The shoulder-rest fits on under the violin, and sits on your collarbone and chest. You should be able to grip the violin comfortably with your chin, so that you can move the left hand freely up and down the finger-board with no danger of the violin slipping about, or your left hand taking any weight. Before the introduction of shoulder-rests, most players used velvet-covered pads fastened to the fiddle with tapes, or slipped under the jacket collar. Some players still prefer such pads. You will have to experiment with various kinds of chin-rests and shoulder-rests in the shop to find which suit you best. A player with a long neck, for example, will need more "packing" to help him grip the fiddle properly than a player with a short neck. Take your own violin with you when buying a chin-rest and a shoulder-rest, because violins vary slightly in depth and shape, and rests that suit you with one instrument may not fit so well with another. When the instrument is supported by the pressure of the chin only, without the left hand, it should feel secure.

The strings wear out and require replacement from time to time. As with the instrument itself, you can pay a lot or comparatively little for strings. The G (4th or lowest) string is always a covered string: that is, it is made of silver or copper wire wound on to a core of gut. The D (3rd) and A (2nd) strings can be plain gut. Many players prefer to use covered strings, aluminium on gut, for these too; but the covered strings cost more. The E or 1st string is almost invariably steel, because gut E strings wear out very quickly. Steel strings change pitch very rapidly when they are tuned, so with a steel string you must have an adjuster or fine-tuner. This is a little gadget that fastens on the tail-piece and enables you to adjust the pitch of the string within fine limits.

Some players prefer a complete set of four steel strings. These strings certainly last longer, and in tropical or humid climates they are essential, since gut and gut-cored strings perish readily. However, the tone of steel strings on violins is generally considered to be inferior to that of gut and covered strings.

Whatever strings you choose, you should ask your dealer to supply you with a matched set. Different makes of strings vary in thickness, and unless the strings are matched for thickness, it is impossible to play fifths – that is, adjacent strings stopped with the same finger – easily in tune.

The Bow

It is as important to have a good bow as it is to have a good violin. When you are doing more advanced bowings, you will rely a great deal on the natural springiness of the bow, and the point at which it balances, to do a lot of the work for you. You will need practice to enable you to choose a good bow, and at first you must rely on the judgement of another player or the advice of a dealer. But there are some things to look for in even the cheapest bow. The stick should curve down towards the hair, and should in fact touch or nearly touch the hair when the bow is slack. The stick must be quite straight from side to side. The nut must fit snugly on the stick, and slide freely. The screw should work easily. Finally, the stick should be lapped or covered at the point at which you hold it, preferably with soft leather or silver wire, to give you a good grip.

The hair of the bow, like the strings, wears out and has to be replaced from time to time. It should present a flat, broad ribbon between $\frac{3}{8}$ in. and $\frac{1}{2}$ in. wide. New hair is clean, white, and free from grease. If the hair of the bow appears old or greasy, the bow will need rehairing before you can use it. This rehairing will have to be repeated at least once a year, and more frequently if you play a lot or use all-steel strings.

Bows, again like violins, vary a great deal in price. If you buy an outfit, a bow will be included. A good bow will cost you from £5 upwards. Unlike violins, bows tend to deteriorate with age. But until it has been tried out, a new bow is something of an unknown quantity, so your best buy is a good used bow, not too old.

To make the hair of the bow grip the strings, you must rub it with rosin. A cake of rosin, properly cared for, will last you for some years. Quality varies, but most makes are perfectly satisfactory. A point to note when buying is that different kinds of rosin are made for 'cellos and violins, so be sure you have the right one. Incidentally, a cake of rosin breaks easily—so do not drop it on the floor if you want it to last.

The Case in which you carry your fiddle should be light but strong. Some cases are made largely of cardboard, covered with cloth. Such a case will afford little protection against rough handling . . . and if you are travelling with a fiddle on buses and trains you are bound to get a few knocks. Choose a wooden-bodied case, plain, veneered, or covered with cloth, with strong hinges and catches. The fiddle should fit snugly but not tightly inside it, and there should be room to wrap the instrument in a silk scarf or cloth to protect it from dust and damp. It is a good idea to have a waterproof outer cover for your violin-case if you intend to take your instrument about much.

Miscellaneous Equipment

A small pair of tweezers is useful when fitting strings. You should always carry a complete spare set of strings in your case, for breakages often happen at inconvenient times. You should have a tuning-fork that gives the note A at concert (new Philharmonic) pitch. At this pitch A equals 439 vibrations a second at a temperature of 68°F. All other strings are tuned from the A string. If you have a piano, you can tune to that—but be sure that the piano is up to concert pitch. If you play a lot, you will find a spare bow an advantage, particularly when you are having one bow rehaired, which can take several days. If you start with a cheap bow and then buy a better one, keep the first bow as a spare. You will also need a mute (see Chapter 2).

The final important piece of equipment is a music-stand. It is perfectly possible to prop music up in odd places to play from, but if you are to stand or sit in the correct position, you must have a music-stand that can be adjusted so that the music is in the right place for you. The best kind of stand to get is an ordinary folding steel stand, which will extend high enough to enable you to read music without stooping when standing up, and will adjust to the right level when you are sitting down. If you travel much, you may prefer a lightweight stand that folds into a small space; but these travelling stands are not so strong as the ordinary kind, and will not support heavy music.

4. Looking After a Violin

Every violin player must know how to look after his fiddle. As with most solo instruments, a violin is a highly personal instrument, and so it needs rather more personal attention than, for example, a piano. Fortunately, all essential maintenance is well within the capacity of even the least practical person. Those with a handy turn of mind will find that certain simple repairs are also well within their capacity, and worth doing, for skilled fiddle repairers are rare and likely to be expensive. They are also generally busy, so that you may have to wait some time for even a minor repair. This chapter deals with the things that every violinist must be able to do; those who want to learn more should turn to Chapter 18.

Storing a Violin

You should keep your violin in a stout case. Inside the case, the instrument should be wrapped in a silk cloth, to protect the varnish and to help ward off damp and cold, two enemies of violins. There is a good scientific reason why a violin dislikes damp and cold. The wood of which it is made is porous; the older the fiddle, the more porous it tends to be. Any damp or cold affects the fibres of the wood, causing them to swell and consequently to vibrate less freely. That is one reason why even a good instrument will on occasion make an atrocious sound. To guard against trouble, you should keep your fiddle in a warm (not too warm) room, away from draughts. If you have central heating, do not leave your violin near a radiator. If you have to take your fiddle out of doors when travelling to play elsewhere, make sure it is warmly wrapped to start with, and that if it gets cold on the journey you get it warm again before you start to play. By warm I mean a comfortable room temperature; some violinists have been known to warm their fiddles in front of a fire, but this can do an instrument serious harm. If you do not play your fiddle for some weeks, open the case and let the violin have an occasional airing. But if you leave a fiddle lying in an open case make sure it is in a safe place where it cannot get knocked, and where nothing can fall on it or scratch it.

Dust and rosin are enemies of the violin; they encourage damp, and also clog the free vibrations of the instrument. The bow scatters rosin on the instrument when you play. Always wipe all the rosin off your violin with a soft cloth after playing. For more elaborate cleaning see Chapter 18.

Fitting Strings

No string lasts for ever, and even strings which have not snapped must be replaced in time, because with wear and age they lose their elasticity, and with it their tone. Metal strings of course last much longer than gut ones, and lose their elasticity much less readily. Make sure that you have the strings on the correct pegs. The two outer strings, G and E, are on the pegs nearest to the nut, and the two inner strings, D and A, on the pegs farthest away. G and D are on one side, and A and E on the other.

To fit a string, remove the old string by slackening the peg, and pulling the end of the string clear of the peg. Never remove more than one string at a time if you can avoid doing so. It is desirable to keep the pressure on the bridge and belly as constant as possible, so that the wood does not have too much settling down to do. The new string will probably have a knot on one end. Some plain gut strings are supplied without knots, and it is then necessary to tie one. Tie a tight double knot near the end of the string, and trim the end so that there is only about a quarter of an inch left. The knot must be small enough to go through the eye hole of the tail-piece, but large enough not to pull through the slot. Slip the knot through the tail-piece and carry the string forward to the peg. There is a small hole in the peg. Push the end of the string through this hole, and pull the end so that you have at least an inch, preferably more, clear. Plait the slack loosely round the string, or tie a half knot in it. Then begin to wind the string on the peg, turning the peg away from the body of the instrument. Wind on in even coils, starting near the hole in the peg and working out towards the side of the peg-box. As you wind on more of the string, the coils will press against the peg-box and tend to force the peg in more tightly, thus preventing slipping.

As tension comes on to the string, make sure that the string is in the little nick on the bridge and in the right groove at the nut. As the tension increases, you may find that the bridge is being pulled forward or even bent. Grip the bridge between the fingers and thumbs of both hands and gently correct this movement. If you do this promptly, the bridge will go back into position without trouble. Note that the feet of the bridge should be centred on the "nicks" of the f-holes.

You may find that the string is not sliding smoothly over the bridge. If so, lubricate the surface of the groove with graphite by rubbing a lead pencil in it—being careful not to mark the faces of the bridge. If you are using covered strings, it is necessary to watch this point carefully, because if the string drags the coils of the covering may tend to open. Many covered strings are supplied with a tiny plastic tube, a quarter of an inch long, to rest in the groove. The string will slide easily through the tube. Make sure that only a millimetre or so of the tube is on the playing side of the bridge, as otherwise it may foul the bow when you are playing near the bridge.

Other points to note with covered strings are: store them straight, or if you must coil them, do so in as big and loose a coil as possible; make sure they are not twisted when you fit them; make sure the knot is big enough to hold in the slot of the tail-piece. If it is not, you can thread the string through the loop which you will find on the knot, and in effect tie the string to the tail-piece. If the covering of a string frays, discard it at once. Not only will it sound bad, but you may hurt your finger-tips on the ends of the wire covering.

With a wire string, you will need an adjuster, which clamps on the tail-piece. The loop on the end of the string will loop over one of the twin hooks of the adjuster. Some strings have a little brass bobbin in the loop; in this case the string passes between the hooks, and the bobbin acts as a stop. Tune the string nearly to pitch with the adjuster at maximum slackness, and then tune the last little bit with the adjuster. A point to note is that the adjuster should be firmly clamped on to the tail-piece, or it may buzz while you are playing. Be sure that the bottom of the adjuster when it is nearly screwed to full take-up does not catch on the belly of the violin. If it does, unscrew the adjuster and take some of the slack on the peg.

Sometimes you will hear a string buzzing. If the string buzzes on every note you play on it, the string is at fault. The gut core has shrunk, and the covering is loose. The only cure is to replace the string. If the buzz occurs on one note only, something on the violin is vibrating in sympathy with that note. See Chapter 18 for possible causes and cures.

A final point on strings: new strings take time to settle down while they lose some of their excess stretch. If possible, never put a new string on less than twenty-four hours before you are due to play in public or with other players, as it will continually go flat (sound lower) until it has settled down. If one string goes badly out of tune, the change of tension on the bridge may cause others to go out of tune also. Covered strings sometimes go sharp (sound higher). Because strings take time to settle, and because the wood of the violin body also has to get accustomed to their pressure, violin strings are never slackened. The violinist should aim to keep his instrument in tune at all times, even when he is not using it.

Care of the Bow

The bow, unlike the violin strings, must be slackened off completely when not in use. Continual tension destroys the springiness of the stick. The correct tension for the bow varies (see Chapter 9). Keep the bow-hair free from grease. The bow will need a fair amount of rosin when it is newly rehaired, or when you have cleaned the hair. At other times, a few rubs before you start to play should be enough. If the bow tends to slip or to squeak, it may need more rosin. If that does not work, the bow needs rehairing. Beware of putting on too much rosin, which will cause the bow to grip the string too much and produce a coarse tone. Never shake the bow, as some players do, to get rid of excess rosin. This can weaken the stick at the head, and result in cracks—to say nothing of the danger of hitting something and smashing the stick. If you have too much rosin on the hair, remove the surplus by drawing the bow over the soft cloth you use for wiping your violin. The stick of the bow should be wiped carefully with the cloth before you put it away.

5. How to Practise

If there is any one secret of mastering an instrument, it is practising the right way. Not just practising: practising the right way. You have probably read how Yehudi Menuhin and other great masters of the violin practised many hours a day, and thought: "How can I ever be any good? All I can manage is half an hour a day." Take courage; a great deal can be done in half an hour of correct practice; and Menuhin's hours of work would have been wasted if they had not been properly used.

Early Stages

The first thing to remember is that regular daily practice is half the battle. Twenty minutes' careful work every day will do far more for you than a four-hour session once a week. You have to strengthen and develop your muscles, just as an athlete or a sportsman does, and train them to react quickly to the instructions of your brain. You have to train your brain to understand and interpret what the music should be. The only sure way to do this is regular, daily, and accurate repetition, building up your skill and your knowledge slowly.

If possible, you should practise for at least an hour a day. But to begin with, you may find that half an hour is enough. As you know, if you suddenly take a long walk when you are not accustomed to much walking, you get tired. Your legs ache, and your feet are sore. But if you walk every day, going a little farther each time, after a while you will be able to walk a long distance and never notice it. The same principle applies to practice in the early stages. If you are beginning to learn the violin, you will be using muscles you do not normally use so much, or in that way. You may easily get tired or cramped.

If you practise when your muscles are tired or cramped, the practice will do you no good. Break off and rest for a while, and then resume. I would recommend beginners to practise for half an hour a day for the first few weeks, and if necessary split up that half-hour into three spells of ten minutes each, with a rest between. After a few weeks, you will find that you can practise for half an hour at a time without any fatigue. Then gradually increase the time you practise, to an hour or more if you can.

To make the best use of your time, divide it up and devote part to each of the things you must practise. Violinists have to learn two entirely different techniques for the right hand and the left hand. For the first few weeks, therefore, beginners should spend a third of their time doing exercises for the left hand without troubling about the right hand. Another third should be spent doing bowing exercises with the right hand, forgetting the left hand for the time being. This will enable you to concentrate on the work of each hand and get it right. Finally, you should spend the remaining third of your time practising fingering and bowing together.

As soon as you can finger the one-octave scale of A major in the first position, you have some finger-work you can use without thinking about it while you practise your bowing. To vary it, you can use the same fingering on the lower strings to play the scales of G major and D major. Conversely, as soon as you can make whole-bow strokes, you have a bowing you can do without thinking while you grapple with the problems of fingering. In this way, you can finger all your bowing exercises, and bow all your finger exercises.

More Advanced Practice

Later on, you should divide your time differently. A good way is to begin with a few finger exercises, followed by a few bowing exercises. Always take a simple exercise, one you know well, first, to get your fingers and bow working. Then practise the more difficult exercises that you are currently working on. After the exercises, play and work at your scales. Again, it is a good plan to play through a scale that you know well before working at the ones you are learning.

After you have practised your scales, you should work at your studies. Studies are pieces of music specially written to develop certain aspects of fingering and bowing. They show you how your early exercises are applied in actual playing. Finally, you come to the piece you are currently learning. A beginner will not be able to tackle pieces for the first few months. Do not worry. The more thoroughly you do your early work, the better you will be able to learn pieces *and get pleasure from them* when the time comes.

The Preliminaries

Most violin practice is best done standing. The body is more free to move in a standing position. However, if you are doing a lot of practice you may wish to do part of it sitting down, because standing up for long periods can be tiring. Whichever you are going to do, begin by putting up your music-stand, and adjusting it to the correct height. It should not be so high that you have to tilt your fiddle up to read the music, nor so low that you are forced to stoop or crouch over the music. Then fit your shoulder-rest or pad to your violin. Next, tighten up the bow to the correct tension (see Chapter 9) and apply rosin to it.

Your next step is to tune the violin. Violinists take the note A to tune to. They take it from some fixed source, in other words, some instrument that does not itself need tuning. If you have a piano, use the A from that, assuming it is up to concert pitch. Tuning to a piano that is not at concert pitch can confuse the ear, and upset the intonation (playing in tune). If you have no piano, it is best to use a tuning fork. A good flageolet—not just a "tin whistle" but a properly-made brass instrument—is an alternative. Get one in Bb; then the note produced when all the holes are open will be A.

Start by tuning the A string. Bow it strongly, while turning the peg with the left hand. You may have to hook a finger or two round the peg-box to give you some purchase. Always come up to the note from below. If you overshoot and get the pitch too high, turn the peg back until you are just below the note, and come up again. The reason for this is that when you slacken off a peg slightly the string may not drop the full amount immediately. But as soon as you start playing on it, the string will go out of tune again.

Make sure that your pegs turn readily, but without slipping. If they slip or stick, you will have to deal with them as described in Chapter 18.

When the A string is in tune, tune the D string to it. Bow both strings together, with a firm, even tone, and bring the D up to pitch in the same way as you did the A. When the D string is tuned, tune the G string to it in the same way. Finally, tune the E string to the A. You may find this a little more tricky, as your left hand will have to curl round to the tail-piece to turn the adjusting screw.

One golden rule in tuning is always to play boldly and to use plenty of bow. If a string is going to stretch or slip, firm bowing is more likely to put it out—and then you can put it right before you begin to play. If you are playing in public, tune your instrument before you go on the platform; any slight adjustments can then be made by bowing quietly or plucking the strings.

A problem for the beginner is how to find the interval fifths between the strings. This is a matter of sheer practice. Listen as much as possible to the sound of fifths. Imagine the sound of Reveille—*doh, soh*. If you have a piano, play fifths on that. Some music shops sell little four-note pitch-pipes which give you all four notes.

A word of warning about the fifths on pianos. Keyboard

instruments are tuned in what is called *equal temperament*.
This means that certain intervals are tuned fractionally
wrong, so that notes that apparently are the same note,
though with different names—for instance, D♯ and E♭—
can in fact be played as the same note. As a result, the fifths
on a piano are the smallest bit flat. At first, you will not
notice the difference. But when your ear has become
trained, you will detect the difference between a correctly-
tuned fifth on your violin and a fifth on the piano.

You should check the tuning of your violin frequently
during practice. It may not vary at all. But on some days
you will find that certain strings tend to go flat frequently.
The amount of moisture in the air and the warmth of the
room you are in will affect the strings. Metal strings as a
rule stay in tune best. Covered strings do all sorts of strange
things. At times they even go sharp.

The Left Hand

Begin your practice with the left hand. Take an exercise
that you know well and play it through carefully. Take your
time over it, no matter how familiar you are with it, in order
to play it accurately. (You will find that when you are really
fluent in an exercise you can play it deliberately—and it
comes out much faster than you realised. That is one of the
joys to be gained from regular practice). This first exercise
is to "warm your fingers up", as you would warm up the
engine of a car. Then turn to the exercise that you are currently working on. Play it through once. See if there are any
passages that are more difficult than the rest—ones that you
stumble over. Repeat these passages several times each,
really slowly, making sure that they are fingered correctly,
and in tune. When you have got the hang of the difficult
parts, put the whole exercise together and play it through
several times, slowly and carefully. Then leave it for a while
and go on to the next exercise, or the next stage of your
practice session.

Why leave it? The mind and body can become wearied by too much repetition all at once, although they will stand any amount of it spread over a period. Leave the exercise to sink into the subconscious. When you come back to it, later the same day or the next day, you will find it just that much easier.

Another important key to successful practising is memorising. When you play something from memory, you have freed your mind of one distraction—looking at and following the music. You are free to concentrate on what your hands and fingers are doing. But there is always a risk of remembering incorrectly; therefore make sure that you memorise accurately. It is only too easy to memorise wrongly, and that means that you are pumping the wrong information into your mind and fingers. In such a case, the more you practise the worse you will play.

After exercises come scales. When you have passed the beginning stage—that is, after the first few months—you will probably be able to start many of your practice sessions with scales. Remember that when you learn a new technique you will have to practise it as an exercise for a few weeks before you can apply it easily and well to scales, studies, or pieces. The remarks that apply to exercises apply equally to scales. Scales are primarily a question of left-hand technique. Practising scales will enable you to acquire speed, and establish the control of long, slow bow-strokes. The various types of scales and how to play them are dealt with in Chapter 12.

The Right Hand

Next, concentrate on the right hand. Bowing exercises are best done on one note, or on a simple scale, which is more interesting. Practise your bowing exercises in the first position to begin with. Many more advanced bowing exercises are applied to special studies designed to give practice and facility in crossing the strings, and in adjusting the bow to the higher positions of the left hand. Learn the left-hand work of such studies off by heart, so that you can forget all about the left hand and concentrate on the bow.

As with the left hand, begin your bowing exercises slowly. Many bowing exercises are complicated patterns of slurred and detached bows. Unless you tackle these slowly at first, you may become confused, and find yourself playing them incorrectly. Bow deliberately, with a full, even tone. Exercises should be played without expression and at first without vibrato. Listen carefully to yourself. If your tone sounds rough, weak, or ugly, stop and try to find out what you are doing wrong. As a rule, poor tone in practice is caused by bowing too timidly, because of unfamiliarity or awkwardness. The cure is simple: play more deliberately and more slowly. Do part of your bowing practice in front of a mirror so that you can see if you are bowing correctly.

Studies and Pieces

Next come studies. Studies are a half-way house between exercises and scales on the one hand, and pieces of music on the other. Most studies are extremely tuneful, and many can claim consideration as pieces of music in their own right. However, they are far more useful for developing technique than pieces are, because studies are specially written to provide repetition of points of technique and difficult passages. As with exercises, the secrets are taking time, taking care, and working at the more difficult parts separately. You should memorise most of your studies if you want to attain real fluency in them.

When learning a new study, play it through once, slowly. If it is a long one, break it into two or three sections, and work at one section at a time. Take the first section, and see which are the difficult bits that you cannot play easily. Work at those as you did with the exercises. You may take a group of several bars, or even one small group of notes, and work at that. Play it as slowly as is necessary to play it accurately. When you have got it right, play a few bars either side of the passage with it to make sure that you link up easily with the parts of the study that you can already play. Then go through the whole study or section. Do not worry if a passage does not come right at once; put it aside and come back to it next day, and the day after that, and so on. Suddenly you will find that you can play the difficult parts of your study as easily as the rest of it. Then polish up the whole study and go on to the next one.

Pieces are learned and studied in the same way as studies. You should memorise all your pieces. However, there is more to learning pieces and the more advanced studies than there is to exercises and mechanical studies. Once you have mastered the technical details, you must start practising the musical side of the pieces. Make sure that you are observing all the marks of expression, and that you have the correct tempo (playing not too fast, as well as not too slowly). Finally, play your pieces as music that you enjoy, and not just as collections of notes.

It is a good idea to have a number of items to practise at various stages of development. You will probably be learning a new exercise at the same time as you are perfecting another. When you are learning new scales, you should also be keeping up some of those you already know. The same thing applies to studies and pieces. Another good word of advice is, do not keep on too long with one thing. After you have practised a study or a piece for a few weeks, put it aside for a bit, even if you have not perfected it, and go on to something else. After a few more weeks come back to the piece you laid aside and work at it again. You will find that it comes more easily to you, and you will get it to a higher stage of perfection more quickly. Never let yourself get stale with practice. On the other hand do not give up too quickly. The great secret is in coming back to the work you have already done. As you learn more difficult things, the ones you have already learned become miraculously easier, and you can play them with enjoyment and confidence.

As you acquire technical skill, there is one other thing to practise that requires repetition of a different sort. This is sight-reading. An ability to play fluently at sight an unfamiliar piece of music is essential for a violinist if he wishes to play chamber music or in an orchestra. Here, the fluency is gained not by repetition of one piece, but by continually reading through unfamiliar pieces. Practise on studies and pieces of a level that you can play comfortably. For example, if you have studied one Handel sonata, you can profitably sight-read the other five.

You will find that it pays to play new pieces through slowly when first practising sight-reading. Play a new piece through at least twice, if only to play the bits you missed the first time. After you have gained some proficiency at sight-reading, aim to keep going. When you are playing with others you cannot go back to get a passage right. You must keep the rhythm. Be very careful over rests, which are a trap to players in ensembles. Count them deliberately—out loud if necessary when you are practising—to make sure that you have not lost the rhythm. You can sight-read the same pieces at intervals of time. If you have not memorised them, they will provide good practice all over again.

Relaxing Exercises

With the best will in the world, you may find that you feel stiff and cramped at times when you are practising. The cure for such stiffness is to do some relaxing exercises. As a rule, the cramp is in the left hand and arm, but you can sometimes get it in the right arm as well. There are two valuable relaxing exercises you can use.

In the first exercise, clench the fist tightly, then shoot the fingers out to open the hand. Repeat several times, and then shake the hand about loosely.

In the second exercise, hold your hands up in front of

you, as if to play a piano or type on a chest-level keyboard. Then let your hands fall forward from the wrists as though you have lead weights in the tips of your fingers. Make sure they fall quite limply. Repeat half a dozen times. Then let the hands and forearms fall from the elbows, again quite limply. Repeat half a dozen times. Finally, raise your whole arms shoulder high and let them fall.

It is a good idea to use the second of these exercises on every occasion after you have finished a spell of practice, and from time to time during a practice session. If you feel the slightest touch of cramp, break off your practice and do one of the relaxing exercises at once. In this way you will avoid stiffening the muscles.

6. Basic Musical Theory

In order to learn any musical instrument well, you must know how to read music. This is easy if you go about it in the right way, and there is not a great deal to learn before you can make progress in studying the violin.

People who write down music have to tell the player two things about each note that he plays: its pitch (how high or low it is), and its length. They do this by writing the notes as dots on a series of horizontal lines called a stave. The stave is rather like a ladder. The position of the dots up or down the ladder tells you how high or low the notes are. The shapes of the dots tell you how long the notes are.

Notes and Their Pitch

The musical stave consists of sets of five lines. These sets of lines are known as clefs, from a French word meaning *key*. Each clef has a sign, which is printed at the beginning of each line. All music for the violin is written in the treble clef, which is printed as shown in Figure 1. The notes are named after the first seven letters of the alphabet—A B C D E F G. The next note after G is A again, because that note sounds like the first A, only higher. The distance between these two A's is called an octave, from a Latin word meaning *eight*, because they are eight notes apart. The distance between any two notes is called an interval, and the chain of notes between a note and its similar note an octave higher is called a scale. The notes of the treble clef are shown in Figure 1. I have written out the scale that begins on C and goes up to another C two octaves higher. You will notice that there are some notes above and below the five lines of the stave. To write such notes, musicians use extra short lengths of lines called leger lines to extend the musical ladder higher or lower when necessary. You will notice also that some of the notes sit between the lines, and some astride them.

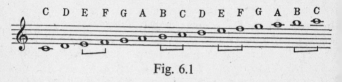

Fig. 6.1

The four strings of the violin are tuned in fifths—that is, five notes apart. The top, or 1st, string is the top E of the treble clef. The 2nd string is A, the 3rd D, and the fourth G. This G below the treble clef is the lowest note that can be played on the violin.

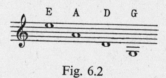

Fig. 6.2

The C on the first line below the treble clef is called Middle C, because it comes about the middle of the range of notes used in ordinary music, and about the middle of the keyboard on the piano. Most of the range of the violin lies above Middle C, and nearly all notes below Middle C in orchestral and chamber music must be played on other instruments, such as the viola or the 'cello.

Those of you who have learnt or tried to learn the piano will know that you can play many tunes using the white keys only, and that most of these tunes end on the note C. These tunes are said to be written or played in the *Key of C*. They can be written down using only the notes in the scale of C, as in Figure 1. Musicians have to vary the way in which they write their notes if they want to write tunes that are in other keys. The reason for this is that, although the scales beginning on any notes are built up in the same way as the scale of C, the intervals between the notes of any one scale are not all equal. The distance between the third and fourth notes, and between the seventh and eighth notes, of the scale are half the distance between any other successive notes. The ordinary distance between two successive notes is called a tone, and the half-distance a semitone. In the scale of C, these semitones occur between the notes E and F, and between B and C. On a piano keyboard it is easy to spot these semitones, because there is no black key between E and F, or between B and C. It is also quite easy to see the difference between tones and semitones on the violin, because you put your fingers down on a string close together for the semitones, and about a finger's thickness apart for the tones. Figure 3 shows the position of the finger-tips when playing the notes A, B, C, D, and E successively on the A string of the violin:

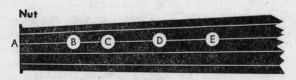

Fig. 6.3

If a composer tried to write the scales of other notes using only the notes he had for the key of C, the semitones would come at the wrong places on the scale. He must alter the way in which he writes the notes so that the semitones come in the right places, that is, between the third and fourth and the seventh and eighth notes of the scale. To do this, he puts signs before certain notes to indicate that they shall be played a semitone higher or lower. A pianist would have to use some of his black keys to play these higher or lower notes. A violinist simply puts different fingers close together on the string. Musicians use a sign called a sharp, ♯, to indicate that a note is to be sharpened—that is, made a semitone higher. They use a sign called a flat, ♭, to indicate that a note is to be flattened, that is, made a semitone lower. If they need to change a note back, or remind the player that it is not sharpened or flattened, they use a sign called a natural, ♮. Sharps, flats, and naturals are placed immediately before the notes to which they apply. Figure 4 shows some more scales, with the semitone gaps in the right places:

Fig. 6.4

It would be clumsy and inconvenient for a composer to keep on repeating the same sharps or flats every time he sharpened or flattened a note when he was writing in a particular key. So he puts the sharp or flat signs that will apply every time in a group by themselves at the beginning of each line of music. By looking at these signs, the player knows that he is to sharpen or flatten certain notes every time he meets them. This group of signs is called a key signature. Each key has its own signature, a different group of sharps or flats. The player merely has to look at the key signature to see what key he is playing in. There is a full table of key signatures in Chapter 12. But in Figure 5 there are three that you should get used to right away—the ones that indicate the scales beginning on the lowest three strings of the violin:

Key of
G

Key of
D

Key of
A

Fig. 6.5

For further information about the various kinds of scales, see Chapter 12.

The Time Value of Notes

There are six main note-shapes to indicate the length of time for which a player holds on a note. Each successive note is half the length of the previous note. In England, the longest note is called a semibreve, and the other notes in descending order are minim, crotchet, quaver, semiquaver, and demi-semiquaver. The American names for these notes are whole, half, quarter, eighth, sixteenth, and thirty-second notes.

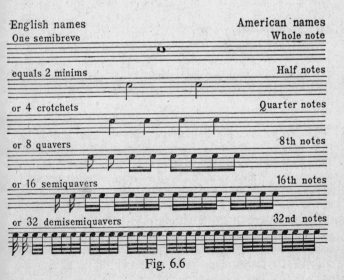

English names   American names
One semibreve   Whole note

equals 2 minims   Half notes

or 4 crotchets   Quarter notes

or 8 quavers   8th notes

or 16 semiquavers   16th notes

or 32 demisemiquavers   32nd notes

Fig. 6.6

In some pieces of music you will see a note with a dot after it, like this: ♩. . The dot increases the value of the note by one-half. Therefore a crotchet with a dot after it equals a crotchet plus a quaver. The table below shows the effect of placing dots after each kind of note:

Fig. 6.7

The shapes of notes indicate the relative lengths of notes, but they do not show the actual lengths of notes. Composers indicate at the beginning of each piece how fast they wish the notes to be played. A semibreve in one piece, for example, might be four times as fast as a semibreve in another. Modern composers often give a metronome figure. This enables the length of a note to be calculated fairly accurately with the aid of a metronome, a clock-like instrument that can be set to tick at varying speeds.

Beats and Bars

If you listen to a piece of music, you will find that it has rhythm. In a march tune, for instance, there is a regular *one, two, one, two*, to which it is easy to walk. These regular accents are called beats. The first beat of each group is always stronger than the others. If there are three beats, as in a waltz, the strong beat is followed by two weak ones. If there are four beats, the strong beat is followed by three weaker ones, but the third beat is slightly stronger than the second and fourth. These groups of rhythmic accents are called bars. They are indicated in written music by drawing

vertical lines across the stave, called bar-lines (see Figure 8).
The close of a piece, or of a section of a piece, is indicated by
a double bar-line.

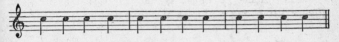

Fig. 6.8

In order to show the number of beats to the bar in a piece
of music, composers put figures on the stave immediately
after the first clef sign and key signature at the beginning of
the piece. These figures are called time signatures. They consist of one figure above another, like a fraction. The upper
figure indicates the number of beats to the bar. The lower
figure indicates the length of note that is to be taken as the
value of each beat. For example, the figures 2/4 show that
there are two beats in each bar, and that the value of each
beat is a quarter-note, or crotchet. Similarly, 3/8 means that
there are three beats to each bar, and each beat is worth an
eighth-note, or quaver. There are two abbreviated time-
signatures in regular use. The time-signature 4/4 is usually
written as C. The C stands for common, and 4/4 time is
called common time, because it is the most common time in
music. The sign ₵ is equivalent to 2/2 and indicates that there
are two minim beats in each bar.

The notes in a bar of music are not necessarily the same
length as the beats. A bar of 4/4 time, for instance, might
contain four crotchets, or two minims, or one semibreve,
or eight quavers, or 16 semiquavers. Or it might contain a
mixture of notes to the total value of four crotchets. All the
bars in Figure 9 contain notes to the value of four crotchets:

Fig. 6.9

Simple and Compound Times

When each beat in a bar can be divided by two—that is, each beat can be represented by two notes of the next smallest value—the music is said to be in simple time. Figure 6.10 shows examples of simple time:

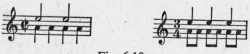

Fig. 6.10

Sometimes composers want to divide each beat by three. Such a time is known as compound time. In such a case, each beat is represented by a dotted note, and each beat can be divided into three notes of the next size smaller. Figure 6.11 shows examples of compound time:

Fig. 6.11

The next table shows the various time-signatures in common use, together with the value in notes of one complete bar. A bar that can be divided into two equal beats is called duple, one that can be divided into three equal beats triple, and one that can be divided into four equal beats quadruple. See Fig. 6.12.

Rests

Sometimes musicians wish to indicate that there is an interval of silence between two notes. Such an interval is called a rest. A rest may last for the equivalent of the shortest possible note, or for many bars. There is a sign for each rest to correspond with each note. See Fig. 6.13.

Table of Time Signatures.

	SIMPLE TIMES		COMPOUND TIMES	
	Time Signature	Value of one bar	Time Signature	Value of one bar
DUPLE	¢ or $\frac{2}{2}$	♩ ♩	$\frac{6}{4}$	♩. ♩.
	$\frac{2}{4}$	♩ ♩	$\frac{6}{8}$	♩. ♩.
	$\frac{2}{8}$	♪ ♪	$\frac{6}{16}$	♪. ♪.
TRIPLE	$\frac{3}{2}$	♩ ♩ ♩	$\frac{9}{4}$	♩. ♩. ♩.
	$\frac{3}{4}$	♩ ♩ ♩	$\frac{9}{8}$	♩. ♩. ♩.
	$\frac{3}{8}$	♪ ♪ ♪	$\frac{9}{16}$	♪. ♪. ♪.
QUADRUPLE	$\frac{4}{2}$	♩ ♩ ♩ ♩	$\frac{12}{4}$	♩. ♩. ♩. ♩.
	C or $\frac{4}{4}$	♩ ♩ ♩ ♩	$\frac{12}{8}$	♩. ♩. ♩. ♩.
	$\frac{4}{8}$	♪ ♪ ♪ ♪	$\frac{12}{16}$	♪. ♪. ♪. ♪.

Fig. 6.12

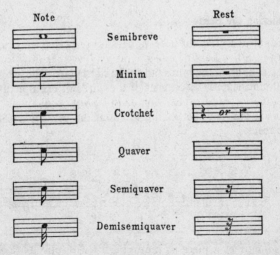

Note		Rest
	Semibreve	
	Minim	
	Crotchet	
	Quaver	
	Semiquaver	
	Demisemiquaver	

Fig. 6.13

Some of the signs are similar in appearance, and may be confused at first. Learn the simple mnemonic "Under, over, right, and left", which will remind you that the semibreve rest is *under* the fourth line of the stave; the minim rest is *over* the third line; the hook of the ᴦ type of crotchet rest goes to the *right*; and the hooks of the quaver and smaller rests go to the *left*. A dot placed after a rest increases its value by half, just as it does for a note. There are special signs for rests lasting more than one bar. (See Figure 6.14). Longer rests are generally indicated by using a sign like a long semibreve rest, with the number of bars' rest in figures above it.

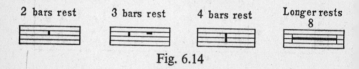

Fig. 6.14

Counting the Beats

With all the different note-values and rests that may be met with in a few bars of music, you may wonder how to keep time so that all the notes fall in the right place. The answer is to count, silently, each beat of the bar. For example, in the first few bars of Corelli's Sonata in B♭ you would count four in each bar—not forgetting to count the beats where there are rests:

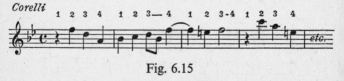

Fig. 6.15

Sometimes a piece of music begins with only part of the first bar. This is a device that composers often use. But they make sure that the piece has a full number of bars in it, by making the last bar short by the balance of the amount of the first partial bar. A piece that begins on the fourth beat of the first bar will end on the third beat of the last bar. You count the partial first bar as though you had already counted the "missing" beats. If the commencing note is less than a whole beat you count the last beat as well (see Figure 6.16).

Fig. 6.16

How Fingering is Indicated

Composers and editors of music use small figures over the notes to indicate which fingers they wish the player to use. The fingers are numbered from one to four, starting with the forefinger. The thumb is not counted. An open string is indicated by a nought. Here is the fingering of the first position:

Fig. 6.17

It will be seen that some of the notes can be played either as open strings or with the fourth finger on the strings below. As you become more advanced you will be able to tell from the marked fingering which of the many positions of the left hand you should be using (see Chapter 7). For example,

is played in the first position

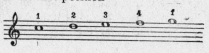

is played in the second position

is played in the third position

Fig. 6.18

A nought with a figure above it indicates a harmonic. Diamond-headed notes with the fingerings for harmonics are artificial harmonics (see Chapter 7).

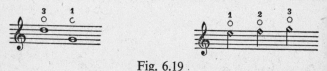

Fig. 6.19

How Bowing is Indicated

The sign ⊓ above a note means it is to be played with a down-bow, and the sign ⋁ indicates an up-bow. For explanations of these terms, see Chapter 9. Notes that are tied together by a slur ⌒ should be taken in the same bow-stroke. Notes not tied together should be bowed separately.

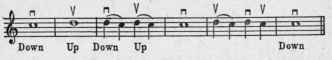

Fig. 6.20

Other points relating to bowing are dealt with in Chapter 9. More points of musical theory are dealt with in Chapters 11 and 12.

Further Reading on musical theory:

Teach Yourself Music, by King Palmer (English Universities Press).
Rudiments of Music, by Stewart Macpherson (Joseph Williams).
The Penguin Dictionary of Music.
The Rudiments of Music, by William Lovelock (Bell).
The Oxford Companion to Music, by Percy A. Scholes.

7. Left-Hand Technique

In the early stages of learning the violin you should study left-hand and right-hand techniques separately. This means that you should be working at Chapter 9 at the same time as this, spending an equal practice time on each. At an early stage you will learn sufficient left-hand technique to be able to finger a simple scale, which you can play while concentrating on your bowing; similarly, you will soon master a few simple bow-strokes to help you with your fingering. Remember that it is easier to hear whether you are playing in tune or not when you bow notes than when you merely pluck the strings.

The following points of left-hand technique must be mastered in turn: the correct way to hold the violin; the position of the left hand; the attitude of the body; the principles of violin fingering; the first position; the third position; glissando; the second position; the higher positions; and vibrato.

It is important to move step by step in this way. You may learn vibrato as soon as your hand is really firm in the first and third positions; any attempt to learn it sooner will unsettle the hand and lead to out-of-tune playing.

HOLDING THE VIOLIN

The Position of the Instrument

The position of the left arm and hand that violinists use is not an obviously natural one. Unless the correct attitude is built up carefully, it is easy to get cramp—with the result that the hand is not free to move easily and quickly about the finger-board. The purpose of the correct attitude of the arm and hand used by violinists is to bring the hand over the finger-board in such a way that all the fingers can reach the strings equally easily, and the fingers can descend on to the strings with the end joints almost vertical.

Nearly all the weight of the violin is taken by gripping it between the chin and the shoulder, as explained in Chapter 3. The tail-piece of the instrument should be just to the right of your chin. The fiddle should project half-left in front of you (see Plate 2). If the instrument is too straight in front of you, you will have difficulty in getting your hand round the neck so that your fingers are over the strings. If the violin points too far to the left, you will find it harder to reach round to bow correctly. The body of the violin should slope slightly from left to right. Make sure that it does not slope too much; it is better to err on the side of having the violin too flat. It is easier to bow lightly if the bow can come fairly straight down on to the strings, using its own weight, than if you have to hold the bow at an angle against the strings.

The lengthwise position of the violin should be nearly at a right-angle to the body. The scroll should be slightly lower than the end under your chin, but only slightly. If the violin droops like a wilting flower, your arm will be cramped between the violin and your chest, and you will not be able to move your hand freely up and down the neck of the instrument.

The Position of the Hand

To bring all four fingers within equally easy reach of the strings, the palm of the hand must be roughly parallel to the line of the violin neck (see Plate 4, Figure A). To avoid cramping the hand, the wrist and arm should be in a straight line, or with the hand bent slightly inwards towards the forearm, and the wrist curving out. Never allow the wrist to bend back so that the palm of the hand touches or approaches the neck of the violin (see Plate 4, Figure B). This position will cramp the hand and restrict its mobility.

Do not allow the neck to drop into the hollow between the thumb and forefinger, or allow the thumb to stick up like a lighthouse above the level of the finger-board (see Plate 4, Figure C). The attitude of the thumb is all-important. It varies according to which string you are playing on, or how high up the finger-board you are playing. In the first position, with the hand near the peg-box, the thumb should be bent inwards at almost a right-angle to curl around the neck. The contact between the neck and the thumb will be midway on the pad when you are playing in the lower positions, and near the tip in the higher positions (see Plate 4, Figure E). The thumb should be approximately opposite the second finger. Some teachers advocate that the thumb should point backwards, towards the peg-box, but this position of the thumb can create tension across the palm of the hand, and hinder the fingers from stretching as widely apart as they need to.

The Position of the Left Elbow

To bring the hand into the position described above, the left arm must come well round in front of the body. The correct position for the left elbow is under the right-hand edge of the violin. At first, this attitude may seem painful, but you must persevere with it until it becomes easy. Remember that the farther over to the right your left elbow is, the more easily can your left hand move about the finger-board to reach the lower strings and the higher positions towards the bridge.

The Attitude of the Body

The violinist can play either sitting or standing. For practising, for playing solos, and for playing duets with a pianist, it is better to stand. The muscles of the upper part of the body can move more freely when you are standing. For

playing chamber music or in orchestras violinists always sit
down. If you are doing a great deal of practice you can sit
down for part of it, particularly for left-hand practice.
It is a good thing to become accustomed to playing sitting
down. Many pupils only play standing up, and do not know
the correct position of the body in relation to a chair.

When standing up to play, the feet should be slightly
apart, at an angle approaching a right-angle to one another
(see Plate 2). The left foot should be slightly in front of the
right foot. Stand upright. Adjust the height of your music-
stand so that you do not have to stoop to read your music.
Your weight should be more or less equally distributed on
both feet, but if you are playing a passage that makes great
demands on your left hand you can put a little more weight
on your right foot so as to free the muscles of your left side.
Keep the body flexible, but do not sway about when playing. You can move your feet a little, but do not move to and
fro; it is distracting to an audience, and does nothing to
help your playing.

When sitting down to play, sit well forward on your
chair, and sit upright or lean slightly forward (see Plate 3).
Do not lean against the back of the chair. Both feet should
be firmly on the ground, the left foot forward, the right foot
back. You will probably have your music-stand relatively
rather farther below eye-level than you do when standing up,
because you need to see over it to watch your fellow players
or a conductor. You may have to lean slightly forward to
read the music. As you lean, the violin will of course droop,
but keep the same angle between violin and body as you
would when playing standing up.

THE FIRST POSITION

The first position is the most important one of all. It is the
position of the hand farthest away from the body, in which
the fingers stop the first four notes up from the open strings.
In this position, the violin has a range of two octaves and a

third. More playing is done in the first position than in any other. Do not attempt to use the bow in the early stages of establishing this position.

The anchor for all the positions is the first finger. Get that placed correctly, and the rest will fall into place easily. Start your practice for the first position on the A string, which is the easiest string on which to learn new techniques. Put the first finger on the string about an inch up from the nut, so that when you pluck the string the note you are stopping is a tone up from the open string. The two joints of the finger should be bent nearly at right-angles, so that the last joint of the finger comes more or less vertically on to the string. The point of contact between the string and the finger is the very tip. You will need to keep the finger-nails of your left hand really short, so that the nail does not make contact with the finger-board and so prop the finger off the string. If it does, you will get a poor-sounding note, probably out of tune. The string must be pressed firmly on to the finger-board. The thumb should be on the neck in front of the first finger, or it may come almost opposite the second finger. Plate 4, Figure A shows exactly how the fingers and thumb should be. Note particularly the straight position of the wrist. Do not let the wrist drop, as in Plate 4, Figure B, and do not let the neck slip into the hollow between thumb and first finger, as in Plate 4, Figure C. The inside of the first finger may lightly touch the neck of the violin from time to time. It is important to remember that, although you apply pressure with the fingers, working against the thumb, to hold the strings down on the finger-board, you do not grip the neck of the violin in order to support the instrument.

When you have established the position of the first finger, put the other fingers on the string. There are four possible groupings of the fingers: with the first and second fingers close together, and the others apart; with the second and third fingers close, and the others apart; with the third and fourth together, and the others apart; and with all four fingers separated. When the fingers are together, they pro-

duce a semitone interval; when they are apart, a tone. As a
first exercise, take the second of these groupings. With the
fingers spaced in this way, you can play the first five notes of
the scale beginning on the open string. You can check the
accuracy of the position of the fourth finger by plucking the
open E string, which should be the same note. You can also
check the accuracy of the position of the third finger by
plucking the open D string, which should be the same note
an octave lower. At this point, make sure that you have
moved your hand round far enough so that the third and
fourth fingers can reach their places easily. If you have any
doubts, move the fingers over to the G string. The greater
reach needed to that string will soon show you if you have your
hand wrongly placed. If the fourth finger persists in going
flat, you almost certainly have the hand in the wrong attitude
in relation to the neck of the violin.

Training the Fingers

When you have established the correct position of the hand
and fingers, you have to train the hand to take up the position
easily and automatically, and train the fingers to move up
and down freely and, above all, accurately. It is important
not to rush this stage of training. You have two aims here: to
be able to put your fingers down firmly and accurately on the
string; and to be able to lift them quickly and cleanly from
the string. Practise putting the fingers down, firmly and slowly,
plucking the string with the right hand to ensure that you have
the right notes. Be sure to keep all the lower fingers down when
using a higher one. In other words, when using the second
finger, keep the first finger down. When using the third finger,
keep the first and second down. When using the fourth
finger, keep all the others down. Keeping the fingers down
is one of the secrets of really good scale-playing and passage work (the playing of rapid notes, such as semiquavers).
    To strengthen the fingers, raise and lower each one ten
times while keeping the others down. At first, you may even

have to help the fingers up with the other hand. As you become more fluent, practise bringing the finger up with a snap. Then practise putting it down sharply, so that you hear a distinct thud as it strikes the finger-board. Then practise a similar exercise as you build up the hand—with the first finger and the open string, then with the second finger while holding the first finger down, and so on. Your violin tutor will have many more exercises of this sort. Practise as many of them as you can, in all four groupings of the fingers. Do not leave an exercise until you have mastered it. Take one or two each day, and practise them. The next day, practise different ones. From time to time, go back and practise old exercises again. When you do, you will realise that progress is being made, because you will find your earlier exercises much easier at the second time of trying them.

Extensions

Extensions are of two kinds: forward and backward. They consist of the movement of a finger beyond the normal limits of the position.

A *forward extension* consists of moving the fourth, or little, finger a semitone up the string—on the A string, to the note F. You will notice that in the fourth of the four groupings mentioned above, the fourth finger does in fact do just that. In this grouping, the third finger is on D♯, so the interval between the third and fourth fingers is a tone. In an extension, the third finger is on D♮, so that the gap between the third and fourth fingers is 1½ tones, or a minor third. This kind of extension is used when you want to play an odd note higher than the position you are in, but do not want to change string or position.

A *backward extension* consists of sliding the first finger back a semitone, for example to B♭ on the A string. In the higher positions the finger may even slide back a whole tone. Again, backward extensions are used to play odd notes without changing string or position.

The Backward First Position

This position involves moving the whole hand as a unit back a semitone. It is essential for playing in the range of flat keys from B♭ onwards. Repeat in this position the exercises that you have been doing in the normal first position.

Note: To prevent undue strain in the early stages, many of your first exercises in the first position can be practised with the violin held across your knee like a banjo. Be careful to keep the correct attitude of the hand and wrist as you would if the violin were held under the chin.

THE THIRD POSITION

When you have attained some firmness and fluency in the first position, it is time to start moving up the finger-board. The third position is the easiest of the higher positions to learn, for two reasons. The first is that the hand has a natural anchoring place for the third position, just as it does for the first position. The second is that the notes of the third position are easy to read, because the odd-numbered fingers —1 and 3—are stopping notes printed on the lines of the stave, and the even fingers—2 and 4—are stopping notes in the spaces, just as they do in the first position.

To find the third position, move your whole hand up the finger-board until the edge of the hand rests against the upper bouts (ribs) of the violin. The thumb sits right in the angle of the neck of the violin. The first finger now rests on the note that the third finger would normally occupy in the first position—on the A string, the note D (see Plate 4, Figure D). From this position, using the groupings of the fingers as in the first position, a whole further range of notes can be reached. On the E string, these extra notes extend the compass of the violin. On the lower strings, the extra notes are of course duplicates of notes that can be played on higher strings. But by using the third position, you can play groups of notes on one string that in the first position you can play only by changing strings. This is the essence of violin fingering technique—placing the hand so that groups of notes fall naturally under the fingers. As with the first position, there is also a backward third position.

To establish the third position, play exercises and studies in that position. Do not attempt to play anything involving moving from the first to the third position and back until you have mastered the next part of violin technique—glissando.

GLISSANDO

Glissando, an Italian word meaning gliding, is the art of sliding from one position to another. In playing, a violinist is constantly changing position, and a careful study of the art of shifting, as it is also called, is an essential for speed and accuracy. You must make all your moves with precision, and know exactly what you are going to do before you do it. In this way, you will change to the right position quickly and silently.

There are three types of glissando: *simple, compound*, and *complex*.

In *simple glissando*, you slide from one note to the next on the same finger; for example, from B to D on the A string.

In *compound glissando*, you slide as before, but add a finger going up or take one away coming down; for example, from B to E on the A string (first finger slides up to D, and the second finger is then put down); or from E to B on the same string (second finger slides down to C, and is then raised).

In *complex glissando*, you slide to a lower finger going up, and to a higher finger coming down. In such a case, you change fingers before sliding when going up, and after sliding when coming down.

The intervening note—the one to which you first slide—in compound and complex glissando is called the *bridge note*. It is also known as the *auxiliary note, intermediate note, gauge note,* or *note of analysis*. In playing, the bridge note should not be heard. In fact, it cannot be entirely eliminated, but can be played so fast and cleanly that it is almost impossible to hear. In your early practice of glissando it is essential that the bridge note should be heard, so that you know that you have made the glide correctly.

You should begin to study glissando the moment you have familiarised yourself with the third position. Begin by practising simple glissando up and down between first and third positions, on all fingers, and on all strings. Then practise compound glissando, by sliding up on one finger, putting down a higher one, sliding back on that, and raising it again. Do this, making use of all possible finger combinations. Finally, practise complex glissando—in going up, lift the upper finger as you begin your slide on the lower one —which then makes the exercise one of simple glissando. Coming down, slide with the lower finger to its correct position, then put down the higher finger. The following examples will make the whole process clear. The tiny notes represent the bridge notes, which are not sounded.

Fig. 7.1

When you have your glissando clear and accurate, try speeding and cleaning it up until you eliminate the sound of the bridge note.

As soon as you have established the correct place on the finger-board for the second position and the higher positions, begin all your work for those positions with glissando exercises. As you learn your scales you will find examples of all three kinds of glissando in them. Work out how they should go, and practise the shifts with the bridge notes audible before you eliminate them. In this way you will achieve clean, fast scale playing with the least difficulty. For further glissando facility, practise also Kreutzer's Study No. 11 in E major.

THE SECOND POSITION

The second position is one of the most difficult to establish— and one of the most useful to be able to use fluently. It lies midway between the first position and the backward third position, and the hand has no anchor point to help you to place it correctly. Careful practise of glissando between first and second positions is the best way to get the position firmly established. Practise slowly, continually checking your intonation by playing the same passages in the first position, or by use of the open strings or a piano.

After the preliminary practice, learn a number of studies written entirely in the second position. They will help to consolidate the feel of the hand in the position. Finally, learn studies that make use of the second position in combination with the first and third positions. At this point you should practise glissando between second and third positions.

THE HIGHER POSITIONS

These are the fourth, fifth, sixth and seventh positions. The fourth, sixth and seventh positions all have a backward position. The fifth position, like the second, does not.

In the higher positions, you will find that the fingers have to be slightly closer together to play the notes in tune. This is because the higher up the string you finger, the shorter the string becomes. A tone or a semitone is a definite proportion of a string; therefore fingers stopping a tone on a short string must be closer than when stopping a tone on a long string. As the hand gets higher up the finger-board only the tip of the thumb remains in contact with the neck of the violin (see Plate 4, Figure E).

Take the positions one at a time, and approach them by glissando practice. You will use more and more of the higher positions as you learn three-octave scales. Gradually you will find that your studies lead you into the higher positions also. It is necessary to be fluent in the higher positions on all four strings, because it is often easier to cross the strings than to change position when playing high passages at a fast speed.

VIBRATO

Vibrato is a musical device that is used to give warmth to violin tone. It is sometimes described as the *close shake*, shake being another word for trill, and this description really tells you what it is. A trill is a rapid alternation of a note with the one above it. Vibrato is in fact a slight sharpening and flattening of the note, producing a throbbing effect. The quality of the vibrato can be varied by altering the amount of sharpening or flattening, and the speed at which it is done.

You should not attempt vibrato until your left-hand technique has become firmly established, and you can finger your notes cleanly, firmly, and in tune. This cannot be too strongly emphasised. Too early a launching into vibrato can unsettle the hand and produce uncertainty of fingering and intonation.

To practise vibrato, begin with the second finger, preferably in the third position on the A string. Put the finger down on the string, and rock it forward, slowly, to sharpen the note slightly; then rock it back until the note is fractionally flat. The finger should roll to and fro on its fleshy tip. The movement comes from the wrist, which must be flexible and in its correct position. Practise the movement extremely slowly at first, bowing the notes, and quickening the pace only when the movement is easy. The vibrato should not shake the whole instrument. When you have mastered vibrato on the second finger, practise it with the others in turn. Pay special attention to the fourth finger—the weakest. Your vibrato must be equally strong on all four fingers, though you will find that a really long note can be held most comfortably on the second finger or the third finger.

Players do not normally have more than one finger down at a time when using vibrato. It is perfectly possible, however, to use vibrato with more than one finger down. Practise it in double-stopping. Avoid letting spare fingers wave in the air when playing vibrato.

DOUBLE-STOPPING AND CHORDS

Double-stopping consists in fingering notes on two strings at once. If you have mastered your early exercises, you will find that having two fingers down on two separate strings is little, if any, more difficult than having them down on the same string. Begin your double-stopping practice with scales in thirds and sixths, which you will find written out, complete with fingerings, in your scale-book. You can use double-stopping to check your intonation in awkward intervals from one string to another. When you play the interval as a chord any out-of-tuneness will be magnified.

With chords, you must finger on three or four strings at once. Chords are written so that one finger can be used on each string, or employing open strings as well. Sometimes one finger is needed on two strings at once. If they are adjacent strings, put one finger down to stop both strings. This chord will be a perfect fifth. You will have to adjust the position of your finger until you get the chord in tune. If your strings are fractionally out of tune, or badly matched (graded for relative thickness), you will have difficulty in achieving perfect intonation. If the same finger is needed on two separated strings, you will have to make another finger do duty. The third finger, for example, can tuck down to play a second finger note if need be.

Care must be taken to see that your fingering is clean, and that your fingers are not touching any strings except the ones they are supposed to. You may have difficulty with the fourth finger, which is inclined to foul an upper string when it is playing on a lower one. The cure is to swing the hand farther round and up over the strings, so that the fourth finger comes down vertically on to the string.

Arpeggios are fingered as chords, but bowed as separate notes.

HARMONICS

Harmonics are a natural phenomenon of vibrating strings. A string actually vibrates not only as a whole, but also in parts—halves, quarters, thirds, fifths, etc. The points of junction between the vibrating sections are called *nodes*. If you touch one of the nodes with a finger, but without pressing the string on to the finger-board, the main vibration will stop, and only the vibration of the parts will be heard. The easiest harmonic to play is the octave. Touch the string lightly with the little finger half-way along its length. You will hear the octave of the open string. If you put the finger right down, you will also hear the octave, but less resonantly. Other harmonics, however, do not occur at the same point as the stopped notes. The double-octave occurs when you touch the string with the third finger in the first position. When you touch the string with the fourth finger in the first position you obtain an octave of the note you would get if you put your finger right down. These are the harmonics most often employed.

Artificial harmonics are produced by stopping the string with the first finger, and then touching the string with the fourth finger. The note produced is the double octave of the stopped note. It is possible to play scales and pieces in harmonics with the aid of artificial harmonics, but it is doubtful whether they have much musical value.

8. Applying Left-Hand Technique

At first, the music you play will be fingered. Your studies and scales certainly will be, and many of your early pieces also. Later on you will come across music with no fingering, or only a few tricky passages marked. It will be up to you to work the fingering out for yourself. Sometimes you will come across fingerings that seem awkward or unsuitable. You must learn how to recognise whether they are really not right, or whether your technique is inadequate to master them. If they are not the best fingerings, you should know how best to adapt them. The beginner should always follow given fingerings, even if they seem strange to him. They are designed for ease of playing or smoothness of effect. The following information will help you to understand how fingering is worked out, and how to finger music for yourself.

General Principles

In most cases the easiest fingering is the best. There are two important exceptions to this rule:

1. If the easiest fingering leads to clumsy bowing, then the fingering should be changed to allow smooth bowing.
2. If the tone contrast of a lower string is needed, then fingering to allow for that should be used.

It should also be remembered that the easiest fingering is not always the most obvious: neither is it confined to the first position.

Broadly speaking, fingering is a matter of grouping notes. For example, four consecutive notes of the scale, if played quickly, will be best played with the four fingers in order. To do this may take you into the second, third, or even the fourth position. If played slowly, the notes may be taken in any position. Remember that the open strings have a more resonant sound than the stopped strings, and that you cannot play vibrato on them. For these reasons you should not use open strings for long notes, though there is no reason why you should not use them in quick passages. In keys with more than one flat or two sharps not all the open strings are available, so it is best to get used to avoiding them.

Remember also that each phrase must prepare for the next, in fingering and bowing as well as musically. If your next phrase is going to take you into a higher or lower position, consider whether you can make the change more easily beforehand or as the phrase changes. Often an apparently isolated high note on the E string, for which the unwary player makes a grab from the first position, can be reached quite easily by preparation—playing the previous phrases on the A and D strings in higher positions that can be reached without difficulty step by step. Similarly, an undignified scramble down the finger-board and up again can often be avoided by crossing the strings, and using the higher positions on the lower strings. Many an apparently tricky passage is in fact a simple one in a higher position. The best way to learn how this kind of fingering is worked out is to watch your studies carefully. They are full of this kind of manœuvre, using apparently awkward positions to make for easy playing. The following notes on some of Kreutzer's studies will help you to understand fingering principles:

1. *Grouping notes so that they lie under the fingers:* No. 11 in E (notice how this study also uses change of position to help smoother bowing); No. 21 in B minor (this one is specially fingered to help trilling);

2. *Using higher positions to avoid clumsy bowing:* No. 29 in D (the opening, in particular, shows the use of higher positions to avoid "leapfrogging" over a string);

3. *Anticipation:* No. 6 in C (in the last few bars, changes of position are made on the A string to avoid wide leaps on the E string).

4. *Crossing the strings* in a higher position to avoid changing position: No. 10 in G (notice particularly bars 13–14–15).

For really fluent playing you should cultivate the often neglected second position. Once you are used to that position you can slip into it easily from either first or third, and can play in it easily many things that are quite difficult in first and third—for example, a two-octave arpeggio in C major. Another useful device, much used by viola players, is a form of "half-position slip"—changing from one position to the next by playing two consecutive notes on the same finger. This is only permissible if it is done cleanly, with no suggestion of a slide.

The Left Hand and Tone

The same note played on the four strings of the violin has a markedly different tonal effect. For this reason composers often use the lower strings to obtain rich, sonorous sounds. An example is Wilhelmji's arrangement of the air from Bach's Suite in D, commonly called the *Air on the G String*, referred to in Chapter 2. In this work, the whole of Bach's flowing melody is played upon the lowest string of the violin. Musicians disagree as to whether this is a successful arrangement or not, but it certainly displays the rich tone of the G string. As a rule music of Bach's period is best played in the lower positions, where the tone of the violin can ring out freely. An example intended by the composer to be played on one string may be found in the slow movement of Rode's Concerto No. 7. A further example, which shows the contrast between notes played in the lower positions and the same passages played in higher positions on a lower string, is Kreisler's *Liebesleid*.

There are no hard and fast rules for such treatment; if the

composer indicates a higher position, use it: if he does not, use your discretion. On the whole, composers of the 1700s made little use of the higher positions for tonal effect. Some later editors of their music indicate the use of higher positions, but in music of the period of Bach and earlier you would be quite justified in using the lowest positions except when the higher positions offered more convenient fingering. When sight-reading it is often better to stay in the lower positions whatever the markings—unless again the fingering is marked for convenience and not for effect.

Vibrato is an important element in tone production. There are two schools of thought on the use of vibrato. Some violinists frown on too great a use of it, and indeed its present-day application to every sustained note is a comparatively modern innovation. A specially clear tone may be obtained by deliberately not using vibrato on certain notes. Violinists occasionally start a long note without vibrato and introduce the vibrato gradually during its length.

On the whole you should use vibrato on every note that is long enough to justify a "warmer" tone. You should always use it on really long notes, but do not attempt it in quick passages except on the occasional long note during the course of a quick passage, which may well be improved by it. Vary the speed and breadth of the vibrato to suit the music, and especially to suit the pitch of the notes. A slow, rich passage on the G string demands a slow, wide vibrato, which would be quite out of place in a passage high up the E string. You should not use vibrato when playing scales or practising tricky passages in order to perfect your intonation. Teachers differ about the use of vibrato in studies, but when you have perfected a study it is natural to use vibrato, and desirable to practise doing so in studies as in other compositions.

Composers generally mark harmonics. It is advisable not to use them in music of Bach's time as it is doubtful whether they were often used in those days. In music of the 1800s, particularly in concertos by the violinist-composers such as Rode, Spohr, Viotti, and de Bériot, harmonics may be employed freely.

Common Faults

Pulling strings. Make sure you put your fingers down straight on to the string. Sometimes players put their fingers down at an angle, and pull the string over towards the palm of the hand. This can result in faulty intonation and is bad for the string.

Hand not far enough round. This most common fault causes notes to go slightly flat on the third and fourth fingers, particularly the fourth, and an inability to reach extensions.

Hand cramped across palm. The cause of this painful complaint is often to be found in the attitude of the thumb. If it is pointing too far back towards the peg-box it creates tension across the palm. Keep the thumb almost opposite the second finger—this will leave the palm free and will also free the hand for a quick move up or down the finger-board. Unless you keep the thumb in this position you will have difficulty in stretches of more than an octave between first and fourth fingers on adjacent strings.

Woolly or strained tone is more often caused by bad left-hand work than by poor bowing. Make sure that your fingers are firmly on the strings. If a string is not properly pressed on to the finger-board the tone will be poor. The "strained" tone is often the result of playing fractionally flat.

9. Right-Hand Technique

Bowing is the hardest part of violin technique to learn. There is a knack to it, just as there is to riding a bicycle, or swimming, or casting a fly when fishing. Once you have the knack, you will never wholly lose it. Like riding a bicycle, bowing a violin is governed by certain laws, and a clear understanding of these laws makes acquiring that apparently elusive knack much easier.

There are three variable factors in bowing: Position, Pressure, and Pace.

Position is the point on the string at which the bow makes contact. If you watch a vibrating string you will see that its vibrations are greatest at the middle, and least at the ends, like those of a swinging skipping-rope. The farther from the bridge and nearer the middle of the string the bow is placed, the more it will tend to damp the vibrations it is itself setting up.

Pressure is the amount of weight applied by the hand to the bow to make it grip the string. If you apply too little pressure, the bow will glide along the surface of the string, hardly making it vibrate at all. If you apply too much, the bow will grip and clutch at the string, producing a sound like the rending of heavy canvas.

Pace is the speed at which the bow travels over the string. It can range from a swift stroke lasting a fraction of a second to one lasting a full half-minute or more.

A fourth factor is the angle at which the bow-hair makes contact with the string. If the hair is flat, so that the whole width is in contact, it will have more grip than if the bow is tilted, so that only part of the hair is in contact. In normal playing, this angle varies according to the part of the bow that is in contact with the string, and to some extent according to the kind of bow-stroke in use. Generally speaking, the hair is slightly tilted when playing near the nut of the bow, where the weight of the hand has the greatest effect; and is nearly flat at the tip, where the weight of the hand is least effective because it is farthest away.

The player has two other controls over the performance of his bow; the tightness of the hair, and the amount of rosin he puts on it. The amount of tension depends on the individual bow, but normally the bow should be tightened so that about half the curve is taken out of the stick. At the centre of the curve, the hair and the stick should be about $\frac{5}{16}$ of an inch apart. This measurement may be a little more or a little less, according to the amount of spring in the stick. Players often slacken their bows a fraction from normal for slow, cantabile movements, and tighten them again for livelier movements in which the spring of the stick will be required. When not in use, the screw of the bow should be slackened off so that the hair is limp, and the stick not in tension at all.

You should apply rosin to the bow before playing. Do not start playing without rosining, unless your previous use of the bow was for a few minutes only. Draw the hair flat over the cake of rosin, and use the cake at all angles, to avoid scoring a deep groove in it. In this way you can use the whole cake. You should be able to see the rosin on the hair as a white powder, but do not apply it too liberally. If you think you have too much rosin on the hair, draw the bow across a clean scrap of velvet. Never shake the bow to remove rosin. You may hit something and smash the bow.

HOLDING THE BOW

The bow-hold has been evolved over the centuries to provide as flexible a contact as possible between the bow and the fingers; to leave the arm, and particularly the wrist, loose and free to manœuvre; and to enable the player to control easily, through the pressure of the first finger (forefinger), the amount of pressure the bow exerts on the string.

The correct way to hold the bow is shown on Plate 7, Figures A and B. The thumb should be bent almost at a right-angle. The tip of the thumb should be placed on the under-part of the stick, close up to the nut, with the knuckle of the thumb touching, or nearly touching, the hair. The second (middle) finger should be on the stick opposite the thumb, and between the tip and the first joint. The bow is in fact held between second finger and thumb. The other fingers then fall into place. The first finger should be clear of the second finger throughout its length. It makes contact with the stick at about the first joint, and the third and fourth fingers at points nearer their tips. The exact position depends on the length and proportions of individual fingers. People with really short little fingers may find that the finger leaves the stick when they are playing near the tip of the bow. They should try to keep the finger on the stick if possible to help to balance the bow. You will find that with the normal bow-hold, the thumb serves as a fulcrum, with the first and fourth fingers controlling the balance of the bow like two people on a see-saw. Pressure from the first finger, as we have seen, controls the pressure of the bow. This pressure is derived not so much from the finger's own muscles as from the wrist and the whole arm, transmitted through the finger.

Once you have established the correct bow-hold, practise it constantly. You can practise it on a pencil in odd moments during the day, until it is quite easy and automatic.

THE BOW ON THE STRING

Now you are ready to put the bow on the string. The length of the bow should always be at right angles to the length of the string. As explained earlier, the bow does dampen slightly the vibrations of the string. If the bow is at a slant on the string it is not only tending to grip a wider stretch of the string, it is also skidding slightly as it is drawn across the string. The result is an unhappy noise. From this you will see that your arm movements must be so controlled that they keep the bow parallel to the bridge at all times. You should do some of your bowing practice standing sideways to a mirror, so that you can check that your bow is in fact parallel to the bridge, and correct it if it is not. See Plate 6, Figure A, for the correct angle of the bow to the string, and Figures B and C for the wrong angles. The exact relationship of the arm to the bow and the strings can best be studied in the context of the whole-bow stroke.

When you are playing a down-bow (marked ⊓) the bow moves from left to right (from the nut to the point in a whole-bow stroke). When you are playing an up-bow (marked ∨) the bow moves from right to left.

THE BASIC STROKES

The Whole-Bow Stroke

The arm takes up three different positions during a whole-bow stroke: at the nut, at the middle, and at the point. It is best to get accustomed to these three positions before attempting to draw the bow across the strings. All preliminary exercises should be done on the A string.

At the nut, the elbow is bent almost at a right-angle, and is below the level of the violin. The first finger forms nearly a right-angle with the stick (see Plate 5, Figure A).

At the middle, the elbow angle has started to open out, and wrist and forearm form almost a straight line (see Plate 3).

At the point, the elbow is nearly straight, and has come forward in order to keep the bow parallel with the bridge (see Plate 5, Figure B). If it does not come forward, the bow will start to travel in a curve—what is called "bowing round the corner". To avoid this curve, aim to produce a curve in the opposite direction, with the bow hand moving away from the body and not closer to it. You will not succeed in producing such a curve—but you will draw a straight bow.

When the bow is at the tip, the first finger lies slightly along the stick as far as the second joint.

You will find that raising the wrist at the nut and dropping it at the point automatically turns the angle of the bow hair slightly. You will find also that the fingers make slight adjustments of position according to the part of the bow that is in use. The one invariable rule is that the position of the thumb and second finger does not change, except as the stick pivots slightly between them.

Now practise whole-bow strokes, slowly, down and up. Put the bow on the string about midway between the bridge and the end of the finger-board, but slightly nearer the bridge. This is the most common position (see Plate 6, Figure E). Count a slow four to each stroke (about one second to each beat, which is slower than you might think). Later you will do whole-bow strokes that are much slower and much faster than this.

One of the most important aspects of bowing is wrist turning. The position of the wrist changes not only according to the part of the bow that is on the string, but also according to changes of direction. When the bow is travelling down, the wrist tends to be slightly depressed, so that in effect it leads the bow down (see Plate 7, Figure C). When the bow is travelling up, the wrist is raised, so that it is pulling the bow up (see Plate 7, Figure D). At the end of each stroke the wrist changes its position. The way in which it changes governs the smoothness or otherwise of the change. If the wrist starts to change from leading one way to leading the other a fraction before the end of the stroke, the change will be smooth and almost unnoticeable. This sort of change is used when playing cantabile (literally, "singing") passages, or when it is necessary to use more than one bow stroke to hold on a very long note. If the wrist change is delayed until after the start of the reverse stroke, the new stroke will have a more definite impact. Such a stroke is often used in playing the detached notes in the music of Bach and his contemporaries.

One of the most difficult things to do is to make the down and up strokes even in tone. Naturally, a down-bow can be given more decision and forcefulness. But music is not written so that it can be played with alternately forceful and less forceful strokes. So you must study to get as much decision into your up-bows as you do into your down-bows.

So far, you have confined your playing to the A string. The movements of the arm are identical for the other three strings, but the whole arm moves up or down from the shoulder. When playing on the G string, the elbow is well up, parallel or nearly level with the shoulder (see Plate 8, Figure A). It drops proportionally for the other strings (see Plate 8, Figures B, C, and D). For the E string, the elbow is about six inches from your right side. Some teachers advocate keeping the elbow well down, but for ease of playing do not be afraid to reach well up and over for the lower (G and D) strings. You will have much better control.

To practise whole-bow strokes, turn to the appropriate exercises in your violin tutor. As soon as you can finger a simple scale, play the scale with really slow whole-bow strokes. Make sure you go right to the end of each stroke, and do not leave two or three inches of bow over. Most people have difficulty in holding out to the end of a stroke, with the result that the last two beats are often of feeble, uncertain tone, with the bow travelling much more slowly than is reasonable. You should aim to play half the note with half the bow stroke. To make sure of doing this, it is best to "save" bow on the beginning of the note. If you are half-way through a note with more than half the bow still to go, it is easy enough to "lose" the surplus. It is difficult to hold out a note with less than the proper amount of bow.

The Forearm Stroke

The second most important stroke to learn is the forearm stroke. This is played using the upper half of the bow, from the middle to the point. The initials U.H. (for Upper Half) are used to indicate it in studies and exercises. As the name of the stroke implies, most of the work is done by the forearm, with the elbow and upper arm remaining more or less stationary. The forearm stroke is in fact half of the whole-bow stroke, and the same points of wrist-turning apply. Practise it at the same speed as you have been practising the whole-bow stroke—that is, counting at the same rate, but only two for each stroke instead of four. This stroke is used for shorter notes than whole-bow strokes, and for bold, deliberate playing at a moderate speed.

The Upper-Arm Stroke

The upper-arm stroke is the other half of the whole-bow stroke, from the middle to the nut. It is indicated by the initials L.H. (Lower Half). Much of the movement for it comes from the movement of the upper arm, swinging from the shoulder. Practise it in the same way as the forearm stroke. It can be used for more weighty playing, but is not so flexible as the forearm stroke.

The Wrist Stroke

The wrist stroke is one of the most useful in the repertory, and it takes many forms. It is the stroke for fast playing, and for linking other strokes together. The stroke is made by keeping the arm still and moving only the wrist, the bow pivoting freely in the fingers. You should practise it in three positions—at the point, at the middle, and near the nut. Each position has its own uses and characteristics.

Near the point, the wrist stroke is used for certain kinds of velocity passages that are too fast for the forearm stroke. In the middle of the bow, the wrist stroke is the basis of the bouncing bow strokes. When the bow is moved rapidly to and fro at the point of balance, it will begin to spring of its own accord. At the nut, the wrist stroke is used for notes that require rather more weight than those played at the point. You should be proficient in work at the nut, because it may happen that the bowing of preceding and following passages will render it essential, for ease of phrasing, to play near the nut.

The wrist stroke, and wrist-stroke techniques, are used for crossing strings. As already explained, the whole arm moves when transferring from one string to another; but for one or two notes this would be clumsy. In such cases, the elevating or depressing of the wrist will enable you to transfer from one string to another. Passages alternating rapidly from one string to another are played entirely with the wrist stroke, or with a wrist flick if they are played legato with a longer bow stroke.

OTHER BOW STROKES

The whole-bow, forearm, upper-arm, and wrist strokes are the basic techniques of bowing. But there are a number of other strokes based on them for producing various kinds of staccato effects. These strokes may be divided into three classes: those in which the bow remains on the string, those in which the bow is thrown on to the string and taken off again, and those in which the bow is made to bounce, either while on the string or by being dropped on to it.

Staccato Strokes on the String

These include the *kick* stroke, the *grand détaché*, the *divided* stroke, and the *following* stroke. The amount of staccato impact varies considerably.

To produce the *kick stroke*, place the bow on the string, and apply pressure through the first finger, so that the stick approaches or even touches the hair. Start the bow stroke rapidly, releasing the pressure almost at the same time. The effect will be as if the violin had "spoken" a note beginning with the consonant K. The pressure is in fact released fractionally after the bow has started to move, so that the bow has a brief grip on the string. You will find by trial the exact moment to take off the pressure. Try this attack with a forearm stroke, and practise it up- and down-bow until you can manage it easily. Then practise it at all parts of the bow. Finally, practise a series of kick impacts in one bow stroke. As you reach the end of each note, lock the bow on the string again, producing a series of notes k ... k... k... k... The kick stroke is also known as the *martelé, martellando, martellato,* or *hammered* stroke. When applied to a whole-bow stroke, it is called *grand détaché.*

The *divided stroke* is a stroke in which two notes are played with one bow stroke, the bow stopping between the notes. The break between the notes may be a slight kick impact, or a fractional lifting of the bow, or just an infinitesimal silence. The *following stroke* is in effect a series of divided strokes in succession. It is used for playing patterns of this sort:

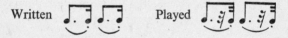

Written   Played

Thrown Bow Strokes

These are played entirely on the lower half of the bow, and usually within six inches of the nut. To play a thrown bow, the hand describes an anti-clockwise circle or ellipse. In the right-hand segment of the circle, the bow is lifted up and forwards; in the left-hand segment, the bow is descending and beginning to move in the direction of the stroke; in the bottom segment, the bow is in contact with the string; coming off at the end of the stroke. The stroke may be played in either direction, but is more usually met with as a down-bow. It can also be played alternately down and up, in which case the hand goes to and fro in a half-circle. The stroke is used for bold staccato passages and detached chords.

Bouncing Strokes

Strokes in which the bow is bounced include *dropped-bow staccato*, *spiccato*, and *ricochet*.

Dropped-bow staccato is similar to thrown-bow staccato, except that it is played near the middle of the bow, and the bow is dropped on to the string and allowed to bounce off again by its own resiliency. It can be played alternately down-bow and up-bow, or with several consecutive notes in each direction. *Spiccato* is produced by using a fast wrist stroke at the point of balance. When sufficient speed has been reached, the bow will bounce of its own accord.

Ricochet bowing is done near the point of the bow. The bow is dropped on to the string with a movement of the hand rather like that of the thrown bow, but on a smaller scale. The hand should be kept well up, so that only the point of the bow moves to any great extent. If you drop the bow on the string in this way, it will bounce a number of times. Try it until you have it bouncing freely without moving the bow along the string. If you then move the bow, you will get a series of fast, crisp, detached notes. Practise down-bow, up-bow, and in mixtures of the two—for example, three notes down-bow followed by one up-bow, all on the same set of bounces.

Crossing the Strings

As already explained, the right arm has four different basic positions for the four strings, and quick movements between two strings can be made with the wrist alone. There are three other cases which involve crossing the strings: double-stops, chords and arpeggios.

Double-stops involve playing two strings together. The arm takes up a position midway between the positions for either string. When playing on two strings at once, it is important to keep the pressure on both strings even. The most usual fault is to play more heavily on one string, with the result that the tone produced on the other string is thin and scratchy.

Chords involve playing three or four strings at once. Since the top of the violin bridge is curved, and the bow-hair is straight, it is not literally possible to sustain a chord on more than two strings at once. (The so-called Bach bow that could play all four at once is mythological, though some have been made in this century to legendary specifications). Chords are played in a spread fashion. For a three-note chord, play the lower two strings together, and swiftly swing the bow over to play the upper two together. The bow does not leave the middle string. For a four-note chord, play the lower two strings together, followed at once by the upper two. In a slow passage, chords played this way will sound slightly spread, but the sound of the lower notes will carry on and blend with the upper ones. Fast or fairly fast chords will sound as if the three or four notes were played simultaneously.

Arpeggios are three-note and four-note chords in which the notes are played separately, but across the strings and not up and down them as in ordinary fingered arpeggios. For such arpeggios, the arm rocks to and fro during the stroke. *Bariolage* is a form of arpeggio playing in which repeated notes are produced using an open string and the same note stopped on a lower string. There is an excellent example in the last movement of Bach's A minor Concerto.

OTHER POINTS OF TECHNIQUE

When starting, the bow may be on the string before it begins to move, in which case there will be a slight kick impact. But if a legato start is required, the bow should begin to move just before it makes contact with the string.

The normal position for the bow is a little less than half-way between the bridge and the finger-board. It can be varied, however, to produce special effects. A bow moved fairly quickly almost over the end of the finger-board will produce a light, carrying tone. This is sometimes called a *floating bow*. It is generally played with *dead-bow weight*— that is, with no pressure at all. Do not try to play over the finger-board with too great a pressure or too slow a pace, or the tone will suffer (see Plate 6, Figure F).

As you play higher up the string with the fingers of your left hand, you can bow nearer the bridge, because you are playing on what is in effect a much shorter string. If you have to sustain a long, slow bow stroke, in any left-hand position, you will find it necessary to move nearer the bridge, and to keep the hair as flat as possible, because you will also need increased pressure to bring out the tone (see Plate 6, Figure D). How close to the bridge you can go depends partly on the instrument. You cannot play really close to the bridge on a bad violin.

The easiest way to increase loudness is to increase the pressure and the pace of the bow, and play nearer the bridge. You can also use either pressure or pace for the same purpose. By varying pressure, it is possible to vary the tone during a bow stroke. Practise this on whole-bow strokes. You should practise going from soft to loud; from loud to soft; starting and finishing quietly with a crescendo in the middle; and starting and finishing loudly with a diminuendo in the middle. In this way, you will attain real mastery of tone production. The same technique can then be applied to shorter strokes.

Harmonics should be played with a fairly light pressure. Too heavy a pressure will break the contact between the string and the finger.

Con Sordino is the use of the mute (sordino) to stiffen the bridge and produce a quiet, veiled tone. You need to play fairly firmly when playing con sordino, even in quiet passages, or the tone will suffer.

Col Legno involves playing with the wooden part of the bow instead of the hair. It is rarely used.

Sul Ponticello means playing with the bow-hair right over the bridge, and with fairly light pressure. The resulting noise is a whistle rather like the wind whistling in the bath-waste. Like col legno, it is rarely used.

Pizzicato

To play pizzicato is to pluck the strings with the fingers. Pizzicato does not produce a very loud tone, as the construction of the violin, unlike that of a guitar, is not suited to this form of playing. But it forms a valuable variation in tone quality. To play pizzicato, put the tip of the right thumb against the top corner of the finger-board nearest to the bow-hand, and pluck the strings with the fleshy part of the right forefinger (see Plate 5, Figure C). Sometimes, the second finger may be used as well. The strings should not be plucked with the nails, as this could damage the strings. Practise pizzicato at first without the bow. To hold the bow for pizzicato, cup the frog of the bow in the hand, holding it against the palm with the second, third, and fourth fingers, leaving the forefinger and thumb free. It is well worth while practising changing rapidly from this position back to normal bow hold, because composers often leave the minimum of time to change back from pizzicato to bowing again. Pizzicato is usually abbreviated to *pizz.* in printed music. A return to bowing is marked *arco*. Pizzicato chords are played by sweeping the forefinger across the strings with a movement of the whole hand, so as to pluck the strings as simultaneously as possible.

Occasionally, pizzicato is played with the left hand. The direction is usually *Pizz. L.H.* Generally, the string is plucked with the little finger of the left hand while the other fingers stop the strings. A descending scale-passage may be played by using all four fingers one after the other, the finger above the stopping-finger plucking the string.

10. Applying Right-Hand Technique

Regular practice of bowing exercises, scales, arpeggios and studies will give you fluency in handling the bow, and familiarity with bowing technique. When practising studies in particular, follow the bowings indicated exactly. They have been carefully worked out both for their training value, and for ease and correctness of performance and phrasing. Once you leave studies and start on pieces, the ground is not so easy to tread, and a number of guide-posts are needed to enable you to find your way.

General Hints

The first thing to remember is that pieces that start on the first beat of a bar (and the third beat in common time) almost invariably begin with a down-bow. A down-bow is more decisive, and launches the piece firmly. If the piece begins on an up-beat (that is, a weak beat, such as a second or fourth beat in common time), you should begin up-bow, ready to play a down-bow on the strong down-beat that follows.

With rare exceptions, all pieces finish on a down-bow, no matter what beat of the bar the last note is on. It is easier to make a clean finish down-bow, and also easier to play a long, sustained note, especially one that dies away.

Down-bows are generally used for chords, but a succession of chords, such as you may find in Corelli sonatas, is often played with alternate down-bows and up-bows. You should practise playing three-note and four-note chords up-bow to cope with such passages.

Long notes present their own problems; if of only one or two bars, they should be played in one bow stroke. If they are longer, they should be broken up so that you can sustain a good tone. Make sure that the joins are as undetectable as you can make them. If you are playing a really loud long note, close to the bridge, you may have to split up even two-bar notes, as you may also if the tempo is extremely slow. An example is the opening sustained G of the slow movement in Bach's Concerto in E; it can be played with one bow, but most players prefer to play it with two. They reverse the normal rule by beginning it up-bow so that the down-bow comes at the beginning of the third bar, as it should.

You may find that, when you vary bowings in this way, your up-bows come on the strong beats. In such a case, you should again vary the bowing to get yourself back in sequence. Do this by splitting two notes that are slurred in the music, or by slurring two notes that are separate. When slurring notes that should sound separate, use a following stroke to provide a break between them.

Generally, music is fully bowed by its composer or its editor. But sometimes editors, particularly those of the last century, apply bowings suited to one kind of music to another kind of music altogether, with results that are not easy to play and not really satisfactory to listen to. The most common mistake is to apply sustained bowings to music of the period of Bach and earlier. In Bach's day, players slurred few notes, and tended to use a separate bow stroke for each note, or to use some of the mixed patterns such as Kreutzer supplies for practice with his famous "Study No. 2." If you find an editor has slurred several bars' worth of short notes together in eighteenth-century music, as if the music were of the Romantic period, do not be afraid to split up his bowings into more manageable sections. However, if he is trying to convey a cantabile effect, be careful not to make your more frequent changes of bow too jerky. In music from the time of Mozart onwards you will find long runs which are meant to be played in one bow stroke. Viotti's concertos contain excellent examples of runs of this sort. If you are playing them up to speed, you should not need to split them. By all means divide them when practising the notes at a slower speed; but do this only for practice.

Bowing marks are generally uniform in their meaning and application. There can be some confusion over apparent staccato marks, though. In music from Beethoven onwards, a dot over a note means that the note is to be played staccato; but in the 1700s, and even as late as Mozart, a dot over a note, particularly a crotchet or a quaver, often merely meant that it was to be played with a detached (separate) bowing, and not slurred. As composers also used dots to indicate staccato, it is necessary to use some care in deciding what is intended. A crisp, detached bow is generally acceptable when in doubt. For music of Bach and his contemporaries detached bowings *should* be crisp; a slight lag in turning the wrist at each change of direction will produce the required effect. Be careful not to overdo the effect, however.

One notable exception to the rule that strong beats come down-bow is found when playing bold passages involving large leaps, sometimes missing a string. You can cross the strings more easily in sequences of this kind by taking the lower note always with the down-bow. If the strong note is on the upper string, play that up-bow, and the weaker note on the lower string down-bow. Mazas's Study, Op. 36 No. 21, provides an excellent example of this bowing, as does Kreutzer's Study No. 7 in D, in which you will see the bowing is reversed in bar 27.

Common Faults

Timidity. One of the commonest causes of poor tone is indecision. If you are sight-reading a passage, do not play timidly. You will make just as many mistakes if you play timidly, and you will sound dreadful as well. Play freely and boldly. The confident method of playing will produce good tone and will help to carry you through technical difficulties with greater ease.

Bowing round the corner is another common cause of poor tone. Watch out for it. If you are constantly producing poor tone, practise in front of a mirror for a while. You will soon see whether the position of your bow is wrong.

Squeaks are due to many causes. Worn bow-hair is one; if in doubt try another bow—your spare, if you have one, or someone else's. Insufficient rosin can also cause squeaks, and so can an indecisive attack. Squeaks on an open steel E string sometimes seem to happen however careful you are. If there are too many of them, and bow and rosin are all right, try a fresh E string, possibly of a different make. Even without changing the string, much may be done by careful and resolute attack. The trouble may be caused by poor fingering, when the strings are not pressed firmly enough on to the finger-board.

That strained sound players sometimes get can be due to many causes. One is using insufficient bow—trying to hold on a note with a bow that is moving too slowly at too light a pressure, or too far over the finger-board. It can also be due to faulty fingering—the fingers either not firmly enough on the string, or even out of tune.

Jerkiness is due to clumsy changing of bow direction. It is something you may not detect unless you hear a tape-recording of yourself. The remedy is to play studies with long, slow bow strokes in them, trying all you are able to conceal the change from one bow to another.

Aggressive ending is a common fault: players bring the last note of a piece or phrase to a fortissimo and abrupt conclusion. Remember that few pieces warrant an ending of this character. Listen to some music by Mozart, and notice how casual his endings often appear to be. Then practise ending the same way. It will soon cure this fault.

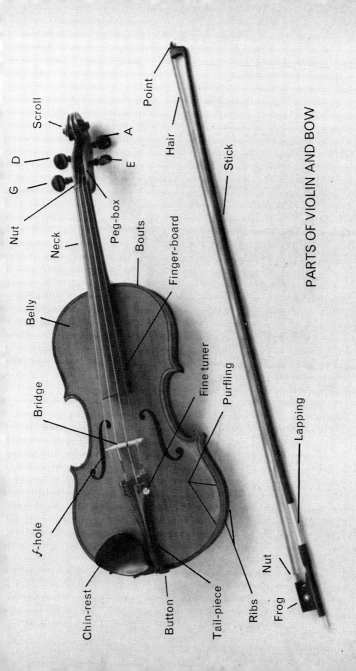

PARTS OF VIOLIN AND BOW

Scroll

A

D

G

E

Nut

Neck

Peg-box

Bouts

Finger-board

Belly

Point

Hair

Stick

Bridge

Fine tuner

Purfling

Lapping

ƒ-hole

Chin-rest

Button

Tail-piece

Ribs

Nut

Frog

Plate 2.   Correct position for playing: Standing

Plate 3. Correct position for playing: Sitting

Plate 4. Attitude of left hand: A, *above*, first position, correct; *Below left*, B, wrong, dropped wrist; and C, wrong, neck in hollow; *Below right*, D, third position, correct, and E, higher positions, correct.

Plate 5. A. *above left*, position of bow-arm when playing at the nut; B, *above right*, position when playing at the point; C, *below*, position of right hand for pizzicato.

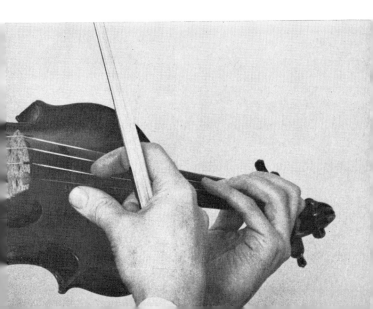

Plate 6. A, *above*, correct contact of bow with string, parallel to bridge; B and C, *below left*, wrong contact, bow not parallel to bridge; D, E, and F, *below right*, bow near bridge, in normal position, and over finger-board.

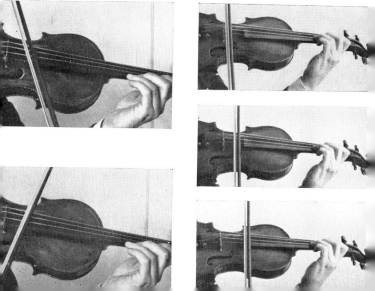

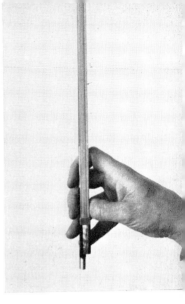

Plate 7. A, *above left*, correct bow hold, top; B, *above right*, bow hold, from underneath; C, *below left*, attitude of wrist, down-bow; D, *below right*, attitude of wrist, up-bow.

Plate 8. Angle of the arm with the shoulder: A, *above left*, on the G string; B, *above right*, on the D string; C, *below left*, on the A string; D, *below right*, on the E string.

Whistling is usually due to playing too fast too close to the bridge. The remedy is obvious.

Grunting is generally caused by playing too slowly with too great a pressure. Again, the cure is obvious.

11. Further Theory

There are a number of further points of theory that the violinist should learn about. They include accidentals, rhythmic variations, abbreviations used in printed and manuscript music, and ornaments. Other essential information is that concerning scales, and that will be found in Chapter 12.

Accidentals

Accidentals are sharps and flats placed before various notes in a piece of music, and are additional to the sharps or flats in key signatures. An accidental indicates a temporary change in a note, and is valid only for the bar in which it occurs. Notes in the next and subsequent bars are not affected. Which accidentals are used depends on what the key signature of the piece is. For example, if a piece is written in C major, a composer puts a sharp (♯) before every note that he wishes to sharpen. But if the piece is in B♭, he can only put a sharp in front of five of the notes of the scale. Two of the notes, B and E, have already been flattened. To sharpen them, he uses a natural (♮), which raises them by a semitone, just as a sharp raises an ordinary note by a semitone. If a composer wishes to cancel an accidental in the same bar (or even contradict it in the next bar, in case the player overlooks the change), he uses a natural for all the notes he has placed a sharp in front of, and a flat for every note he has placed a natural in front of. In a similar way, he uses flats to lower notes by a semitone, or naturals if the notes are already sharpened by the key signature.

If a composer wishes to sharpen a note that is already sharp, he uses a double-sharp (X). If he wants to flatten an already flat note, he uses a double-flat (♭♭). To cancel double-sharps he uses a sharp and a natural together (♯♮), and uses a flat and a natural together (♭♮) to cancel double-flats. Some composers omit the natural, leaving the single sharp or flat to indicate that the note is no longer a double-sharp or double-flat.

Composers use accidentals when they want to modulate—that is, to change key temporarily. They also use them when writing in minor keys. The scale of each minor key differs by only one or two notes from that of the major key a minor third higher. This major key is known as the relative major. Musicians use the key signature of the relative major as the key signature of a minor key, and employ accidentals for those notes that differ from the major key—the seventh note, and sometimes the sixth note, of the scale.

Rhythmic Variations

These consist of changes in the rhythm of a piece from that defined in its time signature.

Triplets are among the most common rhythmic variations. They consist of three notes played in the time of two of similar value, such as three quavers played in the time of two quavers, or of one crotchet. Triplets of this kind are contrary to the general rhythm of the piece; but in pieces in, for example, 6/8 or 12/8 time, the triplets are an essential fabric of the rhythm. *Duplets* (two notes in the time of three) may be met with as variations in triple rhythm.

In 6/8 or similar time, a composer often wishes to tie two notes of a triplet together. In 6/8 time, he does this by writing the two tied notes as a crotchet, and the third note as a quaver, thus: ♩ ♪. But in 12/8 and similar rhythms, he often does it by writing a dotted quaver followed by a semi-quaver: ♪. In eighteenth-century music, and in some later music, this figure is not played as written, with the semi-quaver equal to one third of the value of the dotted quaver, but with the semiquaver equal to half the value of the dotted quaver.

You should be careful to distinguish between the rhythm of a bar in 3/4 time, which you count 1, 2, 3, and a bar in 6/8 time, which you count 1, 2. A passage with six quavers to the bar will sound quite different with the first and fourth quavers accented (6/8 time) on the first time of playing, and with the first, third, and fifth quavers accented (3/4 time) on the second time of playing. Some composers mix the two rhythms in one piece, with some bars counted 1, 2, 3, and others counted 1, 2. There is an example of this in one of Monteverdi's *Scherzi Musicali* for voices and instruments. The way in which this rhythmic variation is written varies; sometimes each change of rhythm is indicated by a change of time signature; at others, the composer simply writes 3/4 6/8 at the beginning and leaves the player to work out by the musical sense which bar is in which rhythm.

Another tricky rhythm sometimes met with is 5/4 time. This may be considered as alternate bars of 2/4 and 3/4 time. Sometimes the stress comes on the first and third beats of the bar, and sometimes on the first and fourth beats. Similarly, 7/4 time may be thought of as alternate bars of 3/4 and 4/4 time.

Syncopation is a common form of rhythmic variation. In syncopation emphasis is placed on beats that would normally be unaccentuated, or the beats are played as rests, with notes on the unaccented parts of the beats (such as the second quaver of a crotchet, the first quaver being a rest). Examples will make this clear. See Fig. 11.1 Passages such as (a) and (b) often occur in ensemble playing, in which case another instrument is generally playing the notes on the beats. In example (c), Corelli gives the player on-beat and off-beat passages simultaneously in a passage of double-stopping. The only way to master syncopation is to count deliberately and steadily. When practising, count aloud if need be.

Fig. 11.1

Musical Abbreviations

Abbreviations are a form of musical shorthand, used to save the composer the bother of writing out a passage more than once. Some abbreviations are rarely met with in printed music, but are used a great deal in manuscript. The following are the more common abbreviations used in violin music.

Repeated passages are marked at the beginning and end by double-bars. The first double-bar has two dots after it, and the second has two dots before it. The dots at the end of the passage indicate that the passage is to be repeated from the last set of dots. If there is no double-bar to go back to, the passage is repeated from the beginning of the piece. Sometimes the ending of a passage is to be played differently on repetition. In such a case two alternative endings are given, one marked 1 (for first time), the other marked 2 (second time). (See Figure 11.2.)

Fig. 11.2

The expression *Da Capo* (abbreviated *D.C.*) indicates that
a passage or piece is to be repeated from the beginning. *Dal
Segno* (*D.S.*) indicates that the piece is to be repeated from
the sign, the sign usually being a form of large S. Sometimes
the repeat is not of the whole passage, but stops part way
through. In that case the stopping point is indicated by a
double-bar and the word *fine* (end).

One kind of movement (section of a musical work) in
which repeats always occur, and generally follow a set pattern, is the *minuet and trio*. The minuet is in two sections,
each of which is repeated. The trio follows, also in two
sections, each of which is repeated. The minuet is then repeated complete, but without repeats of its separate sections.
Scherzos and trios follow similar rules. Occasionally a
composer varies the pattern, but if he does he always
indicates the various repeats clearly.

Repeated groups of notes are indicated thus:

Fig. 11.3

Reiterated or rapidly alternated notes within a bar are often
indicated in this way, one stroke through the stem of a note
indicating quaver repetitions, two strokes semiquavers, and
so on:

Fig. 11.4

Fig. 11.5

A pause is a sign, ⌢ , over a note or a rest (see Figure 6.11 a and b). It indicates that the note or rest is to be held on for a longer period than the strict time of the note. The exact duration of the pause varies with the tempo and character of the piece, and is a matter for the judgement of the performer. A pause sign over a double-bar is often used to indicate the end of a piece, and is the equivalent of *fine* (see Figure 11.6, c). G.P. (for General Pause) indicates that everybody stops playing for the amount of the rests in the bar over which the G.P. is placed, but there is no break in the rhythm (see Figure 11.6, d).

Fig. 11.6

Ornaments

Ornaments are conventional groups or patterns of notes that are used to decorate an otherwise plain passage of music. In the 1700s, composers left a great deal of this decoration to the skill of the performers, merely indicating the form of the ornament by a sign. In some cases, for example the slow movements of sonatas by Corelli, Handel, and their contemporaries, no indication at all was given, and the player was supposed to know by tradition and training what kind of ornamentation to employ and when to employ it. Modern editors of such sonatas generally supply the decorations, or the player omits them in accordance with more modern conventions. However, the use of many classical embellishments has persisted down to the present day, and they occur frequently in music. These ornaments are the turn, the trill, the acciaccatura, the appoggiatura, the mordent, the lower mordent, and—in violin music—the arpeggio.

The *turn* (It. *grupetto*) consists of four notes played after the note over which the sign ∾ is written, but with all the notes within the total time of the written note. The four notes are the note above the written note, the note itself, the note below it, and the note itself again, thus:

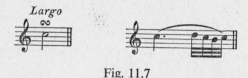

Fig. 11.7

The principal note is held for a large part of its value, but the amount varies according to the speed of the piece. In a slow piece, the principal note may be held for as much as three-quarters of its written value.

The *trill* or *shake* is a rapid alternation of the written note and the one above it, marked by the sign *tr.* over the note, thus:

Fig. 11.8

You will note that the trill ends with a turn. Sometimes this turn is written out as two small notes after the trill note, thus:

Fig. 11.9

The number of alternations varies with the length of the note

and the speed of the music. Sometimes only one or two
alternations are possible, thus:

Fig. 11.10

The turn is often omitted by early composers, and in fast
passages. Generally, the shake should begin with the written
note in music composed since the time of Mozart. For
music by Mozart, Haydn, and their contemporaries, and by
earlier composers, the trill should begin on the note above
the written note, as in Figure 9 above. If the trill note is of
the same pitch as the note preceding it, the trill should begin
on the upper note anyway. An accidental written above the
trill indicates that the upper note is to be sharpened or
flattened.

An *acciaccatura* means a crushing-note. It is written as a
small quaver with a line through it, and is played as quickly
as possible before the note that it precedes, taking little value
from that note, thus:

Fig. 11.11

An *appoggiatura*, meaning a leaning-note, is easily confused with an acciaccatura, as it is written as a small note
without a line through it. You will meet it in the music of
Mozart and older composers. Generally, the appoggiatura is
written as half the value of the note it precedes, and is played
as taking half the value of that note. With a dotted note, it
takes two-thirds of the value. Examples:

Fig. 11.12

Most composers since Mozart's day write the notes out in full-sized notes exactly as they should sound. Editors of some older music have done this, too, for ease of reading and performance. Composers used appoggiaturas to avoid appearing to write discords with the bass of the piece, in times when harmonic rules were stricter than they are now.

The *mordent*, written with the sign ✱ over a note, signifies a single rapid alternation of the note and the note below it. It is more correctly called the *lower mordent*. The upper mordent, written ∿, signifies a single rapid alternation of the note and the note above it. Examples:

Fig. 11.13

Sometimes in music by composers of the 1700s you will come across three-note and four-note chords with the marking over them *Arpeggio*. In such cases, the chords are to be fingered as chords, with all the fingers held down together, but played as arpeggios or open chords, three or four notes up and the same number down (compare the written-out arpeggios in the cadenza of the first movement of Mendelssohn's violin concerto). You will find passages of this kind in many of Corelli's sonatas, and in the great chaconne of Vitali. Most modern editors write out the arpeggio work on a separate stave so that you can see how to play the notes. For example, a minim chord is played as semiquavers, one arpeggio up and one down.

For further information about these and other ornaments, see the entries and tables in *The Oxford Companion to Music* and the entries in Grove's *Dictionary of Music and Musicians*. The application of ornaments is dealt with in *The Interpretation of Music,* by Thurston Dart (Hutchinson).

12. Scales, Arpeggios, and Studies

Scales, arpeggios, and studies are the backbone of a good violin technique. They are also the so-called "dull bits" that nobody wants to practise. But they need not be dull; and if every young player understood their importance in the actual structure and performance of music, as well as in the building of playing skill, there would not be the universal reluctance to practise them.

All music is made up of little patterns, sometimes repeated, sometimes not. Many of these are scale patterns—portions of scales, sometimes a complete scale. The great concertos are full of them. Many patterns are portions of arpeggios: indeed, these are the most common patterns in music. The themes of some of the greatest works are based on them. Examples are the opening movement of Bach's E major Concerto; the cadenza in the Mendelssohn concerto; and the opening phrase for the solo violin in Beethoven's concerto, which is an arpeggio in octaves. If a great many scales and arpeggios lie under your fingers, ready practised, they will "play themselves" when you come to work at your pieces—and you will play the pieces more readily and with less work. Besides, scales and arpeggios rippling fluently off the strings, or played majestically with a rich tone, are rewarding to hear and to perform.

Studies are unfortunate in the name they bear. In fact, they are pieces for solo violin, and some of them are beautiful music. Many of the great piano studies are often played as solo pieces, and there is no reason why violin studies should not be played in that way too. If you want to play by yourself, or to entertain someone when there is no accompanist available, a good study, which is designed to be played on its own, is a far better piece to play than the violin part of a sonata or concerto that all too obviously lacks other parts. The other important point about studies is that they are written to help develop certain points of technique, such as a particular pattern of fingering or bowing. As a result, you will find them much more help in developing technique than you will an ordinary piece of music, which will not be devoted solely or mainly to a particular aspect of violin playing.

Having, I hope, persuaded you that studies, arpeggios and scales are well worth while, and can be great fun to work at, let us get down to a more detailed examination of them and their problems.

SCALES

Major Scales

Some basic scales are described in Chapter 6, with the way in which they are put together. Scales of this kind are known as *major scales*, because the interval between the first note and the third is a major third. A major third consists of two whole tones, one between the first note and the second, and one between the second and the third. There are 12 different major scales. If you play up any string of your violin in semitones until you reach the octave, you will play 12 different notes. Beginning on the A string, these notes are: A, A♯ or B♭, B, C, C♯ or D♭, D, D♯ or E♭, E, F, F♯ or G♭, G, G♯ or A♭. A major scale can be played beginning on each of these 12 different notes. You will notice that some of these notes have two names. Which name is used depends on which scale the note is in. For this reason, some scales can have two names. In practice, the only scales that do have two names are F♯, which is sometimes called G♭, and C♯, which is sometimes called D♭. The notes B, C, E, and F can also have other names, but no scales are called by these names. For example, F can be E♯.

Other Scales

There are three other basic scales that can begin on each note. They are the *chromatic scale*, and the melodic and harmonic *minor scales*.

The chromatic scale we have described above. It is the scale in which every semitone is played. Figure 12.1 shows the chromatic scale of D, beginning on the open D string:

Fig. 12.1

The minor scales are so-called because the interval between the first and third notes of each scale is a minor third. A minor third consists of one-and-a-half tones, a whole tone between the first note and the second, and a semitone between the second note and the third. In the harmonic minor scale, the interval between the sixth and seventh notes of the scale is also one-and-a-half tones. In the melodic minor, the sixth and seventh notes of the scale are played like those of the major scale when going up, but are a semitone lower coming down. Figure 12.2 shows the two kinds of minor scales on the scale of A:

Harmonic
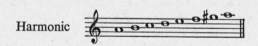

Melodic

Fig. 12.2

When composers write out minor scales, they use the key signature that covers all the sharps or flats except the ones affecting the sixth and seventh notes of the scale. These notes are treated as accidentals (see Chapter 11). In keys with sharps, these accidentals are written as sharps; in keys with flats, they are written as naturals. For further information about the structure of scales, you should consult a good book on theory, such as *Teach Yourself Music*.

A minor scale that has the same key signature as a major scale is called the relative minor of the major scale. The relative minor is always the scale beginning on the sixth note of the major scale to which it is related. Here are the key signatures of the major keys and their relative minors:

MAJOR, AND RELATIVE MINOR KEYS

Fig. 12.3

Learning Scales

On the violin, you must learn the four basic scales for every key—major, melodic minor, harmonic minor, and chromatic. You will find them in your scale-book, written out in two and three octaves. Some of the scales are also written in double notes, and are to be played as scales in two-note chords. Begin with the major scales in two octaves, and do not attempt any of the others until you begin to feel happy about these.

The first scale to learn is that of G major. It begins on the open G string, and lies entirely in the first position. Next, you should learn the scales of A and A♭, which start on the first finger on the G string, and then the scales of B♭ and B, which both start on the second finger on the G string. These scales also lie in the first position.

After this, you will begin to move into the higher positions. Scales are the finest way to become familiar with the positions. The first group in the higher positions are C, which begins on the second finger on the G string and lies entirely in the second position, and C♯, which also begins on the second finger on the G string and lies in the backward third position. By now, you will realise that you can play any scale by starting on the key-note on the G string, preferably on the second finger (which leaves you playing the top note of the two octaves tidily with the fourth finger). But such a starting point is not always convenient for two-octave scales, and so it is better to begin such scales in the first, second, or third positions, changing positions on the E or A strings to reach the higher notes. Your scale-book will give you the fingerings. It may also give some alternative fingerings. Generally, it is best to pick one fingering for each scale that suits your hand best, and stick to it, because you can get the maximum fluency by repeating the same fingerings as much as possible. The scales in which you need to change positions are D, E♭, E, F, and F♯.

When you have attained a reasonable fluency in the major two-octave scales, you can begin on the minor and chromatic scales, taking them in the same order. You will find the appropriate fingerings for these scales also in your scale-book. You will find that the minor scales begin and end on the same fingers as the corresponding major scales. Chromatic scales, however, always begin in the first position, and all the shifting is done on the E string. All chromatic scales are fingered alike up to G♯ (or A♭) on the E string. Starting on an open string, the fingering is 0112234, the first and second fingers being the only ones that play two notes. If the scale starts on any note other than an open string, pick up the pattern at the appropriate finger in the first position. As the scale climbs up the E string, the pattern is 1212 . . . alternately, starting with 1 on the note A. There are two patterns for the last octave of the scale, depending on whether first finger or the second falls on the key-note. If it is the first finger, the fingering is 1212 1212 1233 4; if the second finger, 2121 2121 2233 4. The two patterns are designed to ensure that the scale finishes on the fourth finger. Descending, use the pattern 433221 . . . until a small move brings the hand back into the first position. The E string finger patterns given above fit the two highest two-octave scales, F and F♯, and all the three-octave scales.

When you are fluent in two-octave scales, you can begin to practise scales in three octaves. You can, if you wish, begin learning the first few of these while you are still mastering the last two or three of the two-octave scales. But do not neglect those last two-octave scales in order to rush into the three-octave ones. Begin practising your three-octave scales in the same order as you did the two-octave ones. This time, however, you will find that there are only three sets of fingering to learn, because all the scales from B♭ upwards begin with the second finger playing the tonic (key) note on the G string. Only the scales in G, A♭, and A have different fingerings.

There are two ways of coming down any scale. Two shifts are needed to reach the position in which you started, and the rest of the descent is made across the strings. Some players prefer to make both shifts on the E string; others prefer to make one on the E string and one on the A string. Try both ways to see which you prefer, and having made your choice, stick to it. You may find that having the second shift on the A string, which keeps the two shifts farther part, makes for a smoother run down. But it depends which suits your hand better.

After you have become familiar with the major, minor, and chromatic scales, you will be ready to work at scales in chords, played on two strings at once. Begin with scales in thirds, which are the easiest to get in tune. Always play them firmly and evenly, and do not worry to attain great speed, only great precision. Chords played fast will tend to sound muddy; if you concentrate on really clean, accurate playing, as much speed as you need to match the rest of your technique will develop automatically. Keep the hand well round over the finger-board, and do not let it become cramped (which it will do if you are not careful). At the first sign of stiffness, stop and relax your hand before continuing your practice. After the scales in thirds, practise those in sixths, and then those in octaves. Octaves are played by using the first and fourth fingers together, and shifting the whole hand for each note. Players with extra big hands may try fingering alternate notes 1 and 3, 2 and 4, thus reducing the number of shifts. But most hands are not suited to this fingering. Similarly, players with small hands should not attempt scales in tenths. But scales in harmonics are most useful, and should be attempted by all players who have attained some fluency.

For those who plan to play much modern music, two other scales are useful—the whole-tone scales. There are only two of them, starting on G and A♭ respectively. They are best played by using an extended fourth finger, and shifting up one position on each successive string going up, and down one position coming down. To get high up the E string, play 1212 . . . alternately until the last four notes, which should be fingered 1234. Coming down, reverse the process until the fourth position is reached on the E string: then descend one position on each string until the first position is reached on the G string.

When practising, you should spend as much time as possible on scales. Begin by playing through a number of scales that you already know several times each; then devote the rest of your scale practice time to working on the new scale or scales that you are learning. If your time is limited, always play through at least one of your familiar scales to get your hand in for the session. Aim always at accuracy rather than speed. The speed will come automatically.

ARPEGGIOS

Arpeggios are chords (groups of notes) played in a harp-like fashion, one note after another, instead of all at once, as they can be on a piano or an organ or by several instruments playing together. Violinists learn four kinds of arpeggios.

The *major arpeggio* is based on what is called the major common chord, which consists of the first, third, and fifth notes of the major scale.

The *minor arpeggio* is based on the minor common chord, which consists of the first, third, and fifth notes of the minor scale.

The *arpeggio of the dominant seventh* is based on the chord of the same name, which consists of the fifth, seventh, and second and fourth notes above them of a major scale.

The *arpeggio of the diminished seventh* consists of four notes each a minor third apart.

Arpeggios are best practised with the scales that begin on the same note (which in the case of those on the dominant and diminished seventh are not in the same key). Practise major arpeggios with major scales, and minor arpeggios with minor scales. Play arpeggios boldly: aim to make the notes ring out. A great deal of stirring music is based on arpeggio passages, and if you play your arpeggios in a stirring, bold manner, they will sound like music too. So you will be making music while doing plain, technical practice.

The bowing of scales and arpeggios is a matter of personal preference. But you should bear the following points in mind:

Play each note with a separate bow when learning a scale or arpeggio for the first time;

Next, play scales slurring four notes to a bow, counting two beats on the tonic to make up the number;

When you can play four notes to a bow, play the scales an octave to the bow, again counting two on the tonic;

Finally play all the way up the scale with one bow stroke, and all the way down with another;

For scales in three octaves, play the notes in a triple rhythm, however you are slurring them with the bow. Do not count two on the tonic;

Major and minor arpeggios should always be played with a triple rhythm, ending with a long bow stroke on the lowest tonic note.

Never try to play more notes to one bow stroke than you can comfortably control. In some of the more difficult scales, change the direction of the bow as often as necessary, providing you keep to a regular pattern (in other words, do not change at irregular intervals just because the bow "runs out" there). Practise the more difficult bowings only on the scales that you know best and can play accurately at a good speed.

STUDIES

To begin with, get a book of graduated studies. Such books are selected from groups of studies by many composers and teachers, and generally have notes explaining the particular purpose of each study. Work through this book, and if necessary through other books of a similar kind, until you have reached studies in the third position. You will then be ready to make use of some of the famous books of studies. Two that every violin student should have are Kreutzer's *42 Studies or Caprices,* and Fiorillo's *36 Studies in the Form of Caprices.* Kayser's *36 Studies, Op. 20,* which are designed to prepare the player for Kreutzer's studies, are also well worth having.

Many violin schools and tutors, such as those of Carse and Ševčik, also contain studies. Some studies are aimed principally at the development of left-hand technique, others at developing right-hand technique. Many of the more difficult studies are exercises in combined techniques. The following are some examples of particularly useful studies for developing special points.

Left Hand

Kayser, *36 Studies, Op. 20*: No. 16, for running passages; No. 22, to develop the fingers; No. 27, for arpeggios going into the higher positions.

Fiorillo, *36 Studies*: Nos. 9, 10, and 11, for arpeggio exercise; No. 36, for chords which may also be played as arpeggios (a useful preliminary to Corelli's sonatas); No. 4, for double-stopping (a useful preliminary for Bach).

Kreutzer, *42 Studies*: No. 9, for repeated running passages; No. 11, for position changing; No. 13, for keeping the fingers down; No. 14, for changes of key that might upset intonation.

Right Hand

Kayser, *36 Studies, Op. 20*: No. 19, for quick wrist work; No. 23, for following strokes (and for keeping good tone while wrestling with difficult intonation); No. 24, for speed in passage work.

Fiorillo, *36 Studies*: No. 3, for spiccato; No. 4, for playing passages in chords; No. 8, for long bow strokes with fast left-hand work; No. 23, for passages across the strings.

Kreutzer, *42 Studies*: Nos. 2 and 3 for practising many kinds of bowings in passage-work; No. 4, for kick strokes; No. 7, for crossing the strings; No. 23, for playing a great many notes with one bow stroke.

The above are just a few examples from three of the many books of studies available. You can soon find others for yourself. The books of graduated studies will help you in this. Do not, however, try to run before you can walk. Although Kreutzer and Fiorillo are "musts", approach them gradually, and through books of easier studies. Then when you come to play them, you will not find them daunting—only helpful.

13. Sight-Reading and Memorising

Two things a violinist must be able to do are sight-reading and memorising. Sight-reading enables him to play unfamiliar music straight off. Memorising enables him to play with greater facility and expression music that he has already learned.

Sight-Reading

Sight-reading is the ability to see a piece of music for the first time, and immediately to be able to play it correctly and fluently. Naturally, you cannot expect to sight-read music that is not within your technical capacity. But you should be able to play any music that is within your technical range.

There is a simple secret for sight-reading: deliberate practising of just that. Once you have acquired an ability to play something, even simple pieces, find other pieces of similar difficulty and read a fresh one—or one you have not seen for some time—through every day. Read it through several times, so that you get the tricky parts right. Play each piece as slowly as you like the first time through, and then repeat it up to time. At first, strive for accuracy, not speed, in your sight-reading. But after you have made some progress, you should reverse this order of things. Aim to play what you are sight-reading as nearly as possible up to time, and aim not to break down. If you miss or fluff a passage, keep the tempo going. This is an essential when you are reading chamber music or orchestral music later on. When you are playing with others, you must keep going. If you make a hash of too many passages in a piece at sight, you must practise that piece if you wish to play it, and you must play something simpler or more within your capacity if you wish to sight-read.

The more facility you gain with your scales, and with studies that you are practising regularly, the easier sight-reading will become. You will recognise phrases and combinations of notes, and these will then play themselves whenever you come across them.

Learn to look ahead in your sight-reading. In this way, you can anticipate awkward changes of key or position, and can adjust your bowing to the sense of the music. If you find yourself playing up-bows where the sense tells you you should be playing down-bows, split up two slurred notes or play two detached notes with the same bow stroke to get back into the correct bowing. If you find yourself running out of bow on a long note, change direction without letting the change be heard: but watch ahead for the next phrase, so that you come to it with the right bow. Remember that most pieces end with a down-bow, and plan accordingly. You can find additional material for sight-reading practice in your books of studies; there will probably be some that you are not practising and can read through. You can buy or borrow additional books of studies for sight-reading practice. You can also use pieces for this purpose. Suppose you have learned a sonata by Senaillé. You can try to find others by Senaillé. They are all of much the same difficulty. Do not try to learn them all, but keep them for playing through from time to time at sight.

Memorising

Sight-reading is essential for any violinist who wishes to play with others. Memorising, on the other hand, is the key to learning a piece thoroughly.

You should learn to play from memory the following:

all your scales and arpeggios; your studies, and in particular those studies that you are using for velocity playing and for practising varied bowings (when you know the notes thoroughly, you can concentrate on the variations); and your special pieces, particularly concertos. You should know sonatas well enough to be able to play them from memory, though normally players do use music.

The first and most important rule in memorising is accuracy. You must learn the piece exactly, with the correct bowing and fingering. Do not allow yourself to bow and finger a piece that you are learning one way one day, and another way the next. You will make things much harder for yourself if you do, because your fingers will not automatically go where they should.

There are three ways in which people memorise music: some memorise the appearance of the printed page, and "read" from memory; some rely largely on "finger memory" —a curious mental trick in which the fingers play the right notes automatically once they are set going; and some memorise the sound of the piece, and can play it off in any key. Most players rely on a combination of all three methods, and which they use will be dictated by their own mental make-up and capabilities. It is the subconscious phenomenon of finger-memory that makes it essential always to play a piece exactly the same way as far as technique is concerned.

Take your memorising in small doses. You cannot expect to play a whole piece through several times and remember it. Only a few people have this gift. Take the work to pieces, and practise it section by section, and if necessary bar by bar. Play a small section through several times, and then try to play it with your eyes shut. When you have that piece safely in mind, move on to the next section, and so on. Every so often, put the sections together, to make sure that you have memorised the joins as well as the separate sections. If you want to keep a piece in your memory, keep playing it through. If you neglect it for any length of time, you will probably have to play it through again from the music in order to bring it safely back to mind.

Memorising should not be confused with "playing by ear". That consists of being able to reproduce music that you have heard others play. Some people have this gift more strongly than others. The chief trouble is that you may not hear and remember a piece completely accurately. If you have this gift, do not rely on it too much when you are learning a new piece. Build up your memorising on the sure foundation of accurate playing from the music. Then if your ear is picking up the music, it is from your own careful, accurate reading of the music, backed by correct fingering and bowing.

14. Phrasing, Style, and Interpretation

There comes a time when you can play the notes of a piece of music accurately, in tune, with a good tone, and at the right speed. But this is not enough. How are you going to make the noise sound like music? The answer lies in three words: *phrasing*, *style*, and *interpretation*. A great deal of nonsense is talked and written about all three. They are, in fact, the key to the difference between playing merely the notes as they are written on the music paper, and playing the music that the composer had in mind. There are certain basic things to learn about them that will set you on the right road: and that road is the road to making real music.

Phrasing

Phrasing, in music, is like the formation of phrases and sentences in speaking. When we say something, we stress some words and not others; we pause here for emphasis, hurry there to get something unimportant out of the way; we say some things quietly and others loudly; and we let the pitch of our voices rise and fall to give variety and effect to what we are saying. Music is made up, not just of notes, but of whole phrases and sentences of notes. You have already met one form of musical phrase in the bar, with its simple rhythm and its stress on certain beats. Musical sentences are not divided just by bars. Sometimes they are; sometimes they consist of parts of bars, or of a number of bars.

The rhythm that you found in bars, with their regular groups or two, three or four beats, is found in larger

musical sentences. When composers construct their musical
sentences, they tend (although this is by no means the rule)
to make them four, eight, or sixteen bars long, and to balance
one phrase with an answering phrase. Let us take a simple
example: the hymn "All People that on Earth do Dwell"
set to the tune known as *Old Hundredth* (see Figure 14.1).

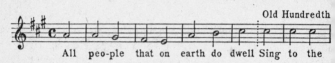

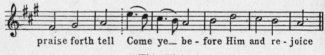

Fig. 14.1

In this version of the tune, each line of the hymn takes three
whole bars, with half a bar at the beginning and the end—
four bars in all. Let us look at the words of the first verse to
see how they will help in phrasing the tune:

> *All people that on Earth do dwell*
> *Sing to the Lord with cheerful voice;*
> *Him serve with fear, His praise forth tell:*
> *Come ye before Him and rejoice.*

Each line is a complete thought in itself. The first is an in-
vocation, the second a command, the two together a command, specifically directed at certain people. The third line
contains two separate commands, linked in sense and in
manner of wording. The fourth line is another command,
clinching the work of the earlier commands. The third and

fourth lines balance the first and second in thought and in verse construction. All four together make a complete set of commands to someone.

Now take your violin and play the tune, thinking of the words and not of the notes. Automatically, you will stress some words and not others; you will let the second line follow the first to form a complete sentence; you will have the two commands in line 3 balancing each other; and the command in the fourth line will round off and clinch the whole verse. Also, you will have in mind that line 1 is leading to line 2; that line 3 is following line 2 and leading to line 4, and that the first three lines are all leading up to line 4.

That was an easy example, because you had words to guide you to the flow of musical thought. Now let us consider a more difficult example (see Figure 14.2). There are no words to help you this time: the example consists of the

Sonata, Op.2, No.8   *Veracini*

Fig. 14.2

opening nine bars of Veracini's Concert Sonata, Op. 2, No. 8. If you analyse the phrasing of the first two bars you will see how you can use variations of the bowing to help towards that phrasing.

The first half of the first bar, with the preceding half-beat, forms a complete phrase, which is repeated in the second half of the bar and in the first part of the second bar. At the same time, notice how the last note of each group of eight notes has a dual function. It marks the end of the phrase, and also serves as the introduction to the next phrase, in the same way that the quaver at the beginning of the whole piece does. The small straight brackets over these phrases indicate these overlaps. The two quavers on the third beat of bar 3 clinch the musical sentence.

Superficially, the three repeated eight-note phrases might appear monotonous. Let us see what we can do with them. There are no words to this piece, but let us put some to it and see how a way of phrasing suggests itself:

> *I'm sure I'm going to win a race*
> (*I'm* sure *I'm going to—win a race*)
> *I'M SURE I'M GOING TO WIN A RACE*
> *TOMORROW.*

The first phrase is a simple statement of a musical idea; the second might be a less confident reiteration; and the third a triumphant assertion, mind made up. You might try the first phrase mezzo-forte, playing the detached notes near the tip of the bow, then the second phrase more quietly, the bow nearer the middle and almost coming off the string on the detached notes, and finally the third and fourth phrases forte, with bold, confident strokes on the detached notes. Notice the little extra stress on the first note of the second phrase ("I'm *sure* . . ."), and the slight hesitation between the two groups of four notes ("going to—win a race . . ."). Try other ways of playing these four phrases; for example, with increasing tone and emphasis, as confidence grows, or with declining tone and emphasis, as confidence weakens;

or as the notes are marked, with the five detached notes of
the third phrase taken with a series of slight bounces in
the same bow stroke, producing a rather more dainty sum-
ming-up of the musical sentence. Now try the same kind of
idea with the next musical sentence (end of bar 2, bars 3, 4,
and most of 5). Notice how the last note of the first sentence,
the B quaver, can also be taken as the first note of the second
sentence. Then play the rest of the example, noting how it
takes in the first sentences and clinches it, with growing
emphasis in bars 8 and 9. Make sure you play those tied
notes in bar 6 down-bow: the emphasis plays itself. Try
playing them up-bow, and see how you have to work to put
the emphasis in. Try, also, playing all those notes in bar 6
with separate bows. You lose the effect of a rising call, and
get instead a stressed note, followed by a weaker repetition
of the note before the stress. Again, in bar 9, try the effect of
slurring the first two notes of each triplet and detaching the
third. Notice how the character of the triplets becomes at
once more dance-like and less bold.

For another example of how bowing can make all
the difference to a musical phrase, look at Figure 14.3.
Notice that the repeated notes are taken with two detached
down-bows. The slight musical hiccup that this way of bow-

Sonata in C

Fig. 14.3

ing gives is in complete contrast to the smooth, rather dull
effect gained by bowing the notes with a down-bow and an
up-bow.

Now for a few general hints on phrasing:

1. If you have a long held note, do something with it—
make it grow louder, or die away, or swell and die away

again; and remember you can do all these things and still keep within an overall *p*, *mf*, or *f* if needed.

2. If you have repeated or answering phrases, do something with them too: play the first loud, the second soft, the first with one style of bowing, the second with a different bowing, and so on. Note: as a rule, answering and repeated phrases sound best played with the same bowing, and the same fingering. If you play an open string the first time, play it again in the corresponding place the second time. But remember, this is a general rule: sometimes you will want to repeat a phrase on a different string (and therefore with different fingering) for contrast. Look at Kreisler's *Liebesleid* for an example of this kind of contrast. The fingerings are Kreisler's own.

3. Think, when you play, of musical phrases, the sentences that the phrases make up, and the paragraphs that the sentences form.

4. Remember that the last note of one phrase may well be the first note of the next phrase.

5. Remember the last beats of your bar: do not skimp or rush them, or you will destroy the rhythm of the piece.

6. Remember your rests, and give them their full value. A well played silence is most effective.

Style

Style in music is basically the convention in which the composer of a particular piece of music wrote it. Style varies according to the period of the music, according to the "school" to which the composer belonged, and often according to the country in which he lived or worked. Style also varies according to the development of the instrument for which a particular piece was written, and the development of the technique of the players at the time it was written. In order to play a piece in the correct style, it is necessary to understand how the composer would have played it, or expected it to be played. A detailed study of musical style is obviously outside the compass of this book, but here are some general hints to guide you in your studies.

In violin music, the first big division of style comes between what is called the Classical School—roughly, music written before the early 1800s—and the Romantic School, which is roughly music from the early 1800s onwards. The Modern School, covering much music of the past sixty years, forms another division. With violin music, the division between the classic and romantic styles coincides with the changes that took place in the structure of the violin, and even more in the structure of the bow, around about 1800. You must remember, however, that all these divisions and dates are arbitrary, and that the transition from one style to another is a long process, with much overlapping. At this point, you should read Chapter 17, HISTORY OF THE VIOLIN, in order to understand how the instrument and its technique developed.

In the earliest days of violin playing, players seldom used any position higher than the third, and their shorter, outward-curving bows were more suited to frequent, smooth changes of stroke than to the long, sustained strokes possible with the modern bow. The music of Corelli is typical of this period. When playing the music of Corelli and his contemporaries, therefore, you should not use high positions on lower strings in an attempt to get variety of tone. The composers did not intend their music to be played in that fashion. Neither should you run long groups of notes together; Corelli used plenty of separate bow strokes to make his music ring out. On the other hand, remembering the softer effect of the Corelli bow, you should be careful not to get too much "bite" into your changes of bow stroke. J. S. Bach, himself a violin-player, extended the range of the violin considerably: many passages in his sonatas for violin alone and his concertos are easy to play only with extensive use of the higher positions. In bowing, however, he relied still on the use of many separate bow strokes.

A point to note is that his three- and four-note chords are "spread"—that is, they are played two and two; the famous "Bach bow" that could play all four strings at once was not invented until this century.

All the music of this period should be played with a reasonable amount of expression, but with the emotional feeling refined down and controlled. The same thing holds good for music of the next period, the late 1700s and early 1800s, exemplified by Haydn and Mozart. But with composers of this period, the bowing is more varied: more groups of notes are slurred, and the higher positions are freely used. Changes of position for the sake of tone quality are proper, and some staccato and bouncing bow strokes are used.

After 1800, the development of the Tourte bow, and the changes in violin structure resulting in longer and more tightly-stretched strings and more arched bridges, led to a great change in technique. The music of Beethoven, Kreutzer, and Viotti shows this change clearly: long runs played with one bow stroke, sustained notes, and a lusher, more passionate style of playing are characteristic of this period. All the fancy tricks of bowing come into their own, together with pizzicato and the use of harmonics, which were rarely if ever used in the music of Bach's period, or even of Mozart's. (If you come across a note that you think you should obviously play as a harmonic in music of the Bach period, the best advice is—don't: play it as a stopped note.) Another device much more used in the music of the 1800s onwards is *rubato*, which may best be described as "bending" the strict time of a piece of music *within a bar*: in other words, you may steal from some notes and give more to others than their strict written values, but always arriving at the first beat of the next bar in strict time.

A vexed question, on which musicologists do not agree, is the use of vibrato. The present-day use of vibrato on every note except in fast passages dates back some sixty or seventy years; before that, some players maintained that vibrato should be used sparingly or not at all. The modern ear is accustomed to the sound of vibrato, and it is doubtful if your Bach would sound any better played without it; however, a wide, throbbing vibrato, suited to Brahms or Tchaikovsky, might well sound out of place in the music of Handel, and you would probably be nearer the usage of the time in employing a more restrained vibrato.

Music of twentieth-century composers is often more aggressive: the bow must sometimes slash at the strings to obtain the harsh qualities of sound that are needed. But much modern music is like that of the 1800s in general style, with all the tricks of tone and bowing employed, yet with an absence of sentimentality that harks back to the Bach period. Fortunately, modern composers are more precise in the marking of their music than their predecessors, and there is less guesswork about their intentions.

Interpretation

Music is a partnership between the composer and the performer. It is generally a remote partnership, in which the one partner has tried to express his intentions on paper in an imperfect form of shorthand, and the other partner has to try to understand what these intentions are. But, just as in an ordinary partnership two heads are often better than one, so it is with composer and performer: the player may be able to add something to the music in the way he plays it that transforms or transcends the intention of the writer.

As we have seen in the section on phrasing, a passage of music may be played in a number of different ways. The task of interpretation lies in choosing which way. One player may see a piece as a dainty, light-hearted composition; another may play the same piece as a bold, forthright declamation. You can try this on the second movement of Handel's Sonata in F Major. The character of this movement changes completely according to which interpretation you choose. Since most indications of speed and loudness are relative, you have some latitude in these two fields. Obviously, you should not try to step outside the composer's written intentions. If he has marked a piece *pp*, you should not play it *ff*. But within the compass he has indicated, you have plenty of latitude. You will be guided by what you know of the style of the composer and his period. For example, you should not try to play Bach with the changes of mood and fancy bowings of a De Bériot *Air Varié*. Here let me add a word of warning about music of the seventeenth and eighteenth centuries. Composers of that time put little in the way of verbal instructions and phrasing marks in their music. The bowings, fingerings, phrasing and dynamic marks in the editions used today are the work of later editors. Some of these editors were great scholars; others tended to impose the ideas of their times on the older music. So if you find, say, a Bach concerto with bowings and fingerings that would not be out of place in a work by Viotti, beware, and try to find an alternative edition and compare the two. Generally, the more modern the edition, the more faithful to the original the editor is likely to be, because modern scholars have been able to make a closer study of old music than their Victorian predecessors.

Finally, let it be said that just as there are many wrong ways of interpreting a piece of music, so there are many right ways; and because A's interpretation pleases you better than that of B, it does not follow that B's is necessarily inferior. Interpretation is, in the last resort, a matter of knowledge combined with personal preference. And it is the performer's share in the creation of music.

15. A Guide to Violin Music

The big problem with violin music is not a shortage, but a glut. The inexperienced violinist is faced with a bewildering choice of pieces of all kinds. Tastes and abilities vary so much that it is impossible to give any hard and fast rules as to what should be attempted, and the purpose of this chapter is to erect a few signposts so that you can find your own way once pointed in the right direction.

Basically, there are three kinds of pieces: the ones that you study to improve your technique and extend your musical range; the ones that you play, with or without a friendly pianist, for your own interest and amusement; and the ones that you play to entertain other people. The three groups are in descending order of difficulty. If you want to gain a reputation for your skill, always play in public only pieces that are well within your capability. You can play such pieces with ease, and devote all your attention to giving a really polished performance. Always if possible play with a piano accompaniment: a solo violin, except in the hands of a good player, does not appeal to many listeners.

Pieces for Violin Alone

Most of the pieces in this class are in fact studies, but they are none the less good music. For performance to entertain others, some of the velocity studies of Fiorillo, Rode, and Kreutzer make good hearing, and you can find many more in the course of your practice that make good hearing. If you do have to play a piece to other people without an accompanist, let it be a study rather than the violin part of a sonata or other work that all too obviously needs an accompaniment. Play whichever of your studies are fluent.

The outstanding works for solo violin are the six suites or sonatas by Johann Sebastian Bach. These are outside the scope of all except advanced players, but when you can play the concertos of Bach and Mozart fluently, you could try some of the easier movements from the suites, such as the Presto from No. 1 in G minor, the Allemande from No. 4 in D minor, the Allegro assai (last movement) from No. 5 in C, and the Gavotte from No. 6 in E. But do not attempt these movements until you can practically play them at first sight.

Pieces for Violin and Piano

Most music publishers issue albums of simple, tuneful pieces, graded according to difficulty and according to the left-hand positions used. These pieces offer the best introduction to violin and piano playing. Many of them, however, are arrangements of familiar airs and melodies from works not originally written for the violin. It is more satisfactory to move on to the simpler classical sonatas, and to the many simple pieces written specially for young violinists. There are many other pieces for the violin that require only a limited left-hand technique, such as one or two of Kreisler's lovely melodies, but most of them need the ability to play long, sustained bow strokes with a good tone.

Sonatas.

The best sonatas to begin on are those by composers of the 1600s and 1700s, who were writing at a time when violin technique was less advanced than it became in the 1800s. An excellent series of these sonatas by a wide range of composers was edited by Alfred Moffat, and they are published by Simrock.

Among the best sonatas of this period are the six by

George Frideric Handel. The easiest to start with are No. 3 in F and No. 6 in E. Other sonatas of only moderate difficulty include those by Jean Baptiste Senaillé, Francesco Maria Veracini, Lorenzo Somis, and Prospero Castrucci. Archangelo Corelli wrote twelve sonatas that should be in every violinist's repertoire. Of these, Nos. 7, 8, 9 and 11 are moderately easy. The rest contain a number of passages in double-stopping that require a greater technique. Giuseppe Tartini's Sonata in G minor, known as the *Dido Forsaken*, is of about the same difficulty as the more advanced Corelli sonatas. Most of Tartini's other sonatas are much harder, as are the violin and clavier sonatas of J. S. Bach. These sonatas of Bach are an exception to the general rule of the day in that Bach wrote out the whole of the keyboard part. They are most rewarding to play, and so are his six flute and keyboard sonatas, which transfer well to the violin.

Of later sonatas, those by Wolfgang Amadeus Mozart should be readily playable by anyone who has mastered Corelli. They are true duets for violin and piano, whereas in most of the earlier sonatas mentioned above the keyboard player has a subordinate part (the Bach sonatas being an exception). No. 1 in A, No. 4 in E minor, and No. 10 in B♭ are recommended to begin with. Franz Schubert's three sonatinas (which are really sonatas) are of comparable difficulty to Mozart's sonatas. Ludwig van Beethoven's Sonata Op. 24 in F (the *Spring Sonata*) is of about the same difficulty, but his other sonatas require a much more advanced technique. His *Kreutzer* sonata is one of the greatest virtuoso works for the two instruments. People who can play the more difficult Mozart sonatas can also tackle the sonatas of the nineteenth-century composers Edvard Grieg and Robert Schumann, and possibly those of Johannes Brahms. Most of the many fine sonatas of the twentieth century require an advanced technique, and some of them pose problems of intonation because of the awkward intervals in them.

Concertos

A number of violin concertos are often referred to as "teaching concertos" because teachers use them for training their pupils in advanced technique. Few violinists have a chance to play such concertos with an orchestra, but many of them are quite satisfactory to play with a piano accompaniment. The solo parts are more rewarding for solo practice than sonata parts, because they are generally more complete in themselves. The following concertos are recommended out of the many available, and are graded in approximate order of difficulty:

Antonio Vivaldi: Concertos in A minor, A major, and G minor (and many more). These concertos form a good introduction to the classical style of the 1700s.

Pierre Rode: Concertos No. 7 in A minor and No. 8 in E minor. These concertos form a good introduction to the romantic style and the bravura concerto.

J. S. Bach: Concertos in A minor and E major. The concerto in D minor, better known in its piano version, is a magnificent work, but requires a much more advanced technique.

Jean-Baptiste Viotti: Concerto No. 22 in A minor.

Rodolphe Kreutzer: Concerto No. 13, in D.

Mozart: Concertos No. 4 in D and No. 5 in A.

The great concertos of Beethoven, Felix Mendelssohn, Brahms, Max Bruch, Peter Tchaikovsky, and Jean Sibelius require a great deal more technique, and should preferably be studied under the guidance of a teacher. But there are many more concertos by Vivaldi, Rode, Viotti, Kreutzer and Mozart, and also concertos of varying difficulty by other composers of the violin-virtuoso school, such as Charles de Bériot, Tartini, Pietro Nardini, and Henri Wieniawski.

Other Pieces

Other pieces for the violin include simple melodies, often arrangements, and bravura works designed to show off the player's technique. Kreisler's *Classical Manuscripts* in the style of various composers include some works of only moderate difficulty, such as *Liebesleid*, *Preghiera* (Padre Martini), *Aubade Provençal* (Couperin), and *Sicilienne and Rigaudon* (Francoeur). Most of his other works call for much greater technique. Other simple or fairly simple pieces include Francis Thomé's *Simple Aveu*, Anton Dvorak's *Humoresk* (many versions, that edited by Kreisler being in a difficult key), Bach's *Air on the G String* (an arrangement by Wilhelmj of an air from the Suite in D), Charles Gounod's *Ave Maria*, and Joachim Raff's *Cavatina*.

You should attempt at least some of the bravura works to extend your technique. Recommended to start with are Charles Dancla's *Romance and Bolero*, Op. 50, De Bériot's *Airs Variés* (particularly No. 7), Kreisler's *Praeludium and Allegro, Liebesfreid,* and *Schön Rosmarin*, and Edward German's *Bolero* in E.

Music for Two Violins

Many of the composers of studies have written duets for two violins, among the best known being those by De Bériot, Jacques Féréol Mazas, Rode, Kreutzer, Ignaz Joseph Pleyel, and Ludwig Spohr. The most enjoyable duets for two violins, however, are those with piano accompaniment. They include many classical trio-sonatas of the 1600s and 1700s, particularly those by Corelli, Handel, Vivaldi, Henry Purcell, and William Boyce. Most of these trio-sonatas were written with a continuo part for keyboard and 'cello. Where possible, you should buy editions with optional 'cello parts.

There are also a number of concertos for two violins. Bach's concerto in D minor is one of the greatest violin works, and his concerto for violin and oboe can also be played on two violins. Vivaldi and Corelli also wrote enjoyable double concertos. All these double concertos can be played with piano accompaniment.

16. Playing with Others

The violin is essentially a sociable instrument. It can, of course, be played on its own: there are many fine compositions for violin alone, and a few master works of great technical difficulty, of which the six sonatas of J. S. Bach are incomparable. But the violin is at its best when playing with other instruments, and that is one of its great advantages, for making music on one's own is never so satisfying as playing in company with others. Concerted music is also one of the best ways of making, and keeping, friends.

There are two ways in which an amateur violinist can make music with others: in chamber music, as a member of a duo, trio, or larger group; and as a member of an orchestra. Although duet playing with a piano is strictly chamber music, it is sufficiently different from other forms of chamber music to deserve a section on its own, especially as it is usually the first form of chamber music that a young violinist plays.

PLAYING WITH A PIANO

The Music

Every violinist should try to play duets with a pianist as early in his playing career as possible, and however simple those duets are. Apart from its musical satisfaction, playing with a piano is the greatest possible help in learning to keep in time and in tune—two points on which the novice violinist generally has the most difficulty and needs the most help.

In some works, the piano plays a supporting role to that

of the violin. Its part is in every sense of the word an accompaniment. The classical sonatas of the late 1600s and the 1700s are typical examples of this kind of combination. Many of these sonatas were written as solo violin parts with a figured bass. The figured bass was a kind of musical shorthand: the composer wrote down the bass line, which is generally the second most important part of any piece of music after the tune (the exception being where the bass itself is the most important part). Over each note of the bass, the composer wrote figures to indicate the harmony he wanted, according to a code still used for identifying chords in textbooks and teaching. Keyboard players in those days were accustomed to improvising a complete keyboard part from this kind of skeleton. Your pianists, however, will not have to exercise their skill at improvising. Modern editors have realised (written out) the figured bass parts for all the well-known and some not so well-known eighteenth-century violin music. There is not, unfortunately, an equal degree of skill in the way this work has been carried out. For example, Handel's six sonatas as realised by Arnold Dolmetsch (Novello) have splendid piano parts, which complement the violin part instead of providing just a background and harmony. Some other editions, however, have much simpler and extremely dull keyboard parts. When you are buying such music, take a pianist with you to see if the piano parts are well carried out.

With later music, this problem does not arise. Composers wrote their keyboard parts out in full, and often made the piano very much an equal partner with the violin. (Mozart's eighteen sonatas are in fact described as for piano and violin, and not the other way round.)

The Team

So much for the music: now for the teamwork. Try to find a pianist with whom you can play frequently, if not regularly. As a beginner, you will find an advantage in having an accompanist of greater skill than yourself, who can help you with the sense of the music, and also help you to keep an ear on your intonation. You need, too, someone who knows how to *accompany*—that is, someone who will not insist on playing a piano solo with violin obligato. Too many pianists, trained in solo playing, have this fault. If you can find someone who genuinely likes ensemble playing, you are in luck.

In the early days of your musical career, you should play only pieces that the pair of you have practised separately. Your purpose is to make music together, not to try to solve technical difficulties while the other partner waits. You should have practised enough to be able to finger all the notes fluently, and to be able to play any fast or tricky passages at a reasonable, *and constant*, speed. Nothing confuses a pianist more than changes of tempo for which the composer did not call. In an allegro movement, pick the hardest passage, and see how fast you can play it without stumbling. Then make that speed your speed for the whole movement.

One problem for beginners is how to start together. At first, one of you may count a "bar for nothing" to set the tempo. When you have played a piece once, and know the tempo, this should be unnecessary. Later, you should learn to set the tempo silently. This is the task of whichever instrument starts, or the solo instrument if both start together. The pianist has your part as well as his own written out in front of him, so he can see what you are doing as well as what he should be doing. This gives him a great advantage. It also means that he is better placed to follow someone else's lead.

To lead, you must stand where the pianist can see you. As you go to play your first note, give a slight nod of the head—in fact of the whole fiddle—to mark the beat before the one on which you start. If the piece begins on the first beat of the bar, your silent beat will be the last beat of the previous bar. If you begin on the last beat of a bar, or the last half-beat, you will give the previous beat, or the first half of the last beat. Make your movement really slight: you do not want a wild gesture that will distract or amuse anyone watching. But make it clear-cut and obvious. You can make a definite movement without making a big one.

It may be, of course, that the pianist will start. A nod of his head as he begins will indicate to you when he is going to play, and if you have any length of time to wait before you come in, you should begin counting silently to yourself so that you know exactly when the violin part should start.

While you are playing, you must listen carefully to what your partner is doing. Your two parts must fit like a glove on a hand. You will find phrases in one part are answered in another. Listen, too, for the harmony; it will help you to pick out the climaxes and cadences (closes) in the music, and to shape your part to fit. It will also help to prevent you from getting lost, and, if you do stray, to get back without breaking down. Listen carefully for the first beat of each bar: generally the pianist will have it if you do not. If you are playing syncopated passages off the beat, listening for the beat will assist you to fit your off-beats in easily.

In addition to learning how to be accompanied, you must also learn how to accompany. Sometimes the piano has the main part, and the violin plays a supporting role. You will find this often in Mozart's sonatas—for example, in the opening of No. 10 in B♭. In such passages, you must let the pianist have the floor, and fit your part to his.

This brings us to one of the most vexed questions of duet playing—loudness. The pianist can obviously make far more noise than you can. He must learn to keep his volume of tone lower than he would for similar markings if he were playing solo. At the same time, you must learn not to play so softly that he cannot help but drown you, or so loudly that he has to bring his tone up to match, regardless of the composer's dynamic indications (when to play loudly or softly). Careful attention to the markings will help a lot here. The effect when you reach a crescendo together, or a sudden pianissimo, is worth all the effort. An inexperienced accompanist will have more difficulty over dynamics than you will. If he persists in playing too loudly, stop and insist that he moderates his tone, pointing out tactfully that you are playing a duet in equal partnership.

Learning Together

Now for some hints on how to practise together. For a new piece, a run-through first, to get the feel of the thing, is a good idea. The run-through will also give you a fair indication of which passages are the most difficult to play together. Then take each movement, section by section, in the same way that you have practised it on your own, and play it through together, repeating tricky passages until you are both thoroughly familiar with them. Finally, put the whole piece together, and play it through without stopping. If you have practised a piece thoroughly beforehand, it may not take you long to reach the final stage. Sometimes you may need several rehearsals, with individual practice of some passages, before you can play a piece well together.

More advanced players often sight-read a fresh piece together, for fun or to find out what it is like. Even then, they can do more with it if they wish. They can try the piece through, then practise their parts individually. Or they can polish up a piece that they are sight-reading then and there, if it is well within their technical capabilities, by going through it in the way described above, but without the preparatory individual practice. It is a good rule not to leave a piece that you have tried through without trying to overcome any difficulties with a short and careful rehearsal of the tricky parts.

A pianist can also help you when you are learning and practising concertos. You need to study a number of concertos in order to learn how to apply points of technique. All the great and not-so-great concertos are published with piano versions of the orchestral parts. Your pianist may object to playing long *tutti* (orchestral) parts, particularly long introductions. In such cases you can agree on cuts. Some editions of concertos have optional cuts marked, usually by two signs like this: ⊕ The player omits the bars between the two signs.

PLAYING OTHER CHAMBER MUSIC

The Various Groups

Basically, chamber music is music for small groups of instruments, designed to be played in a chamber or room, rather than a massive piece to be played by many instruments in a large hall. The music, however, may still be on a grand scale emotionally and structurally. The most important kind of group for the string player is the string quartet. Composers have also written string quintets, and sextets, septets, octets and nonets; quartets and quintets with one or more wind instruments; and trios, quartets and quintets with the piano as one of the instruments. Also in the chamber-music class are the trio sonatas written by many composers of the 1600s and 1700s. As these trio sonatas are likely to be the first chamber music that the young violinist will play after duets with a piano, we shall consider them first.

Trio Sonatas

The sonatas known as trio sonatas were generally written for two solo instruments with a continuo. *Continuo* meant a continuous bass part, usually with a fingured bass like the early violin sonatas. The continuo part was played on a harpsichord or other keyboard instrument, with a 'cello or viola da gamba (an instrument similar in range to the 'cello) reinforcing the bass line. The 'cello part was needed because harpsichords could not sustain notes. A modern piano has better sustaining power, so it is in order to dispense with the 'cello if need be. But if a 'cellist is available it is better—and more fun—to play the sonatas as they were written.

Many trio sonatas were written to be played on a variety

of instruments. The solo parts could be played on two violins, or two flutes, or a violin and an oboe, and many other combinations, including treble and tenor recorders. So, with a sonata of this kind, you can vary the solo parts according to what instrumentalists you have available. Flute, oboe, or recorder will blend well with the violin in music of this sort. You may have to experiment in order to find out which instrument sounds better playing the upper part. Generally a recorder should play upper parts because its tone is weak; flutes and oboes can play either. Purcell, Corelli, Handel, and Telemann all wrote sonatas for two violins, and there are many more by less well-known composers. There are also a number of early double concertos that can be played with a piano accompaniment, particularly those by Bach and Vivaldi.

String Quartets

All string quartets are written for two violins, viola, and 'cello. The members of the quartet play together as a team, but a special responsibility rests on the first violin. He acts as leader; he sets the tempo, and generally gives the signal to begin playing. When tuning, the first violin should tune his instrument first, to a tuning-fork or a piano. The other instruments should then tune, in turn, to the pitch of the leader's violin.

Seating is important. When playing on their own, quartets generally form a square; the first violin faces the 'cello, with the second violin on his left and the viola on his right. If an audience is present, the players sit more in a half-circle, with the leader on the left from the audience's point of view. Keep your stands low enough so that you can watch each other over the tops of the music.

String quartets are the most rewarding form of chamber music. If you have been accustomed to playing with a piano, you will find the transition not difficult. However, there are many differences.

First, you must learn even more to play a subordinate part when that is your role, and to play out when you have a solo passage. Remember that each part in a quartet, however dull it may seem, is vital to the music as a whole. Listen to the whole quartet, not just to your own part. The dullness, if any, of your own part does not matter, because you are contributing to the complete sound.

When you begin quartet playing, you will undoubtedly play the second violin part. Do not mind that, even if the first violin—in Haydn quartets particularly—seems, like the Devil, to have all the best tunes. Your part is just as vital. The second violin is frequently playing duets with someone else—now with the first violin, now with the viola, now with the 'cello. At times he is leading a string trio that is accompanying the first violin. At others he is providing a firm foundation on which the first violin can execute all those airy arabesques that sound so delightful. And because the second violin part is often (though not invariably) technically less exacting than that of the first violin, you will have more time to enjoy the music and get used to quartet work.

When you are practising a quartet it is useful to have a miniature score of the work handy, so that you can see how the parts are supposed to fit together.

The leader gives the signal to start in just the same way as described when playing with a piano, with a slight nod of the head. But the leader does not always have the start, either at the beginning of a movement or after a pause or cadence during it. In that case, whichever instrument has the lead-in gives the cue. You will find it a good rule to keep an eye on your colleagues, as well as an ear. It will help you to fit your parts together—a particularly useful point when dealing with answering phrases. Try to match your phrasing of similar passages, in style of bowing particularly. Try also to match your tone. If one instrument is playing legato, while the others are playing similar parts detached or boldly, the result will sound unmusical, even though the notes are correct.

When rehearsing, it is best to play a movement through first, to get the feel of it and earmark difficult passages. Then work through it, practising the tricky sections until all the parts fit together properly. If you can practise your parts separately in between meetings, so much the better. The first violin usually leads the rehearsal, stopping the quartet when things go wrong, and deciding what passages need repetition or changes of balance or phrasing. Since a string quartet is essentially team-work, it is up to any member of the quartet to make constructive suggestions. Here let me say that one of the most important qualifications for the four members of a quartet is compatibility. If they get on well together, they will play together better than a group with perhaps greater technical accomplishment but less mutual understanding. In a temperamentally matched quartet the better players help the weaker ones because they enjoy making music together.

String Quintets

Quintets for strings may be written for two violins, two violas, and 'cello; or for two violins, viola, and two 'cellos. Some people feel that the string quintet is not so well balanced musically as the quartet. But quintets are just as much fun to play, and all the remarks that apply to quartet playing apply to quintets too.

Strings and Others

Piano trios and quartets have some of the qualities of piano duets, and some of those of string quartets. The violinist is still the leader, but in keeping the ensemble together and in helping rehearsals the pianist can be of great assistance. He has all the parts in front of him, and can tell what should be going on, even if it isn't. Whereas in string quartets and quintets the essence is a blending of tone, in groups with a piano the composer generally uses the percussive qualities of the piano as a foil to the blended sound of the stringed instruments. As with duet playing, the pianist must learn not to drown his fellow players. In all works with a piano, the string players tune their instruments to the piano.

Other combinations may include one or more wind instruments, particularly a flute, oboe, clarinet or horn. The instruments with a more powerful tone should be blended in carefully to match the string tone. The string players should tune their instruments to the wind instrument, which cannot be varied much in pitch. Some music of the eighteenth century is written for groups in which some parts may be played by either violins or wind instruments. An example is Telemann's Quartet in F for recorder, violin, oboe, and continuo ('cello and keyboard), in which the oboe part may be taken by another violin, and the recorder part by a flute. There are also groups including a lute or a guitar, notably quartets for string trio and guitar by Paganini, and at least one written partly by Schubert.

Trios for strings are usually scored for violin, viola, and 'cello, though there are some for two violins and 'cello, and Dvořák and others wrote for two violins and viola.

PLAYING IN AN ORCHESTRA

Playing in an orchestra can be rewarding. There you have an opportunity to meet and learn from other players. If you have a good conductor he will make you play well music that you thought was beyond you. This will be good for your technique and your morale.

One of the most important requirements in orchestral playing, even in an amateur orchestra, is discipline. If you undertake to play, make sure you attend all the rehearsals, arriving promptly. Make sure you have mute and rosin handy, and spare strings in your case. If you are given music to practise on your own, practise it, and especially any difficult passages. You must bow and phrase passages as they are marked, or as the conductor tells you. The bows of a section of violins must move as one. Have a pencil handy to mark changes of bowing or fingering. Pay great attention to intonation: it is the hardest thing to achieve in orchestral playing, and the most noticeable blemish. Keep a good, singing tone, even in quiet passages. Too many amateur orchestral players forget to use their bows freely, and produce unhappy-sounding scratches instead of soft, carrying tone in quiet passages.

In most orchestras, you share a stand, called a desk, with another violinist. The pair of you should work as a team. If you are with an experienced player, he will help you through difficult bars. Do not lean on him unnecessarily, though. Count your own rests, and do not rely on him to give you your cues to come in. The violinist on the left of each pair (as they face the conductor) should turn over the music, using his right hand to do so. Sometimes the parts are split. In such cases, the music is marked *divisi* (divided), and is generally, but not always, written on two staves. The violinist on the right, who is the leader of the pair, takes the upper part, and his partner the lower part.

Besides watching the music, you must learn to watch the conductor. In practice, you keep half an eye on him, in much the same way as a car driver keeps half an eye on his rear-view mirror while still looking where he is going. The conductor gives you the beat and the dynamics. He cues your entries, and by his gestures indicates how he wants his players to phrase the music.

A final word of warning on orchestral playing: if you play a great deal in orchestras, make sure you keep your standards of technique up in your practice sessions and other playing. One among a crowd of players cannot be heard— you probably cannot hear yourself too distinctly—and bad habits of sloppy intonation and bowing can go undetected for a long time. Amateurs are particularly prone to lapse in this way. As a corrective, try quartet playing: any faults will show up all too clearly.

Books for Further Reading

The Art of String Quartet Playing, by Herter Norton (Simon and Schuster, 1962).

The Well-Tempered String Quartet, by B. Aulich and E. Heineran, translated by Craig (Novello, 1938).

The Playing of Chamber Music, by George Stratton and Alan Frank (Students' Music Library: Dennis Dobson, 1951).

17. History of the Violin

Every student should know something about the history of the violin, because violin music was composed at all stages of the instrument's development. It is easier to play music well if you know the circumstances in which it was composed—the way in which people played at the time, and the stage of development that had been reached in instruments and technique. For example, a great deal of music that is rewarding for the amateur player was written more than 200 years ago, when violins were not quite as they are now, and techniques of playing were different. Allowances for these differences must be made in playing the music today. The history of the instrument will make clear the reasons for some of the stylistic variations discussed in Chapter 14.

The Background

Musicians have used instruments with strings for many thousands of years. Harps were played in ancient Egypt and Greece. The lute, a plucked instrument with a neck and several strings, was known at least 2,000 years ago. Bows were used as instruments in their own right by primitive men, but it is not known when stringed instruments were first played *with* bows. The first bowed stringed instruments that we know about developed sometime between A.D. 800 and A.D. 900. These early fiddles had many names, such as rahab, rebec, lyra, or hu-ch'in, according to the countries in which they were played. Musicians played fiddles in lands from China across Asia to Morocco and other parts of North Africa, and in Europe. Many of these instruments

ad apparently little in common with a modern violin,
part from the fact that they had strings, a sounding-box,
nd a neck, and were played with bows. By the 1300s,
owever, recognisable violin shapes are traceable, in old
anuscript drawings, in carvings that decorate old
urches, and in paintings. Many of the primitive kinds
f fiddles that preceded these early violins have survived
to modern times as folk instruments in Asia, Africa, and
urope.

By the late 1400s and early 1500s, two forms of fiddle had
olved in Europe. As far as we can tell, some had been
ossed in construction and in manner of playing with
tes and guitars. Instruments of this first kind were held
pright on the knee, and bowed somewhat like a modern
ello but with the bow held underhand. They also had frets—
at is, raised bars across the finger-board for the more
curate stopping of notes, such as a modern guitar has.
hese frets, however, were made of loops of gut, and were
us technically movable frets, such as some Asian instru-
ents have today. This first kind of fiddle was called a viol,
d it was made in many sizes. Viols remained popular for
out 300 years.

The second kind of fiddle was possibly a direct descend-
t of instruments of the rebec type. Instruments of this
nd were held on the arm, or under the chin. Because of the
gle at which they were held, their players evolved an over-
nd bow-hold. These fiddles had no frets. In time, they
olved into the violin family. To distinguish the two kinds
instruments, people in Italy—then the centre of the great
ltural revival known as the Renaissance—called the fiddle
ayed on the arm the *viola di bracchio*—viola of the arm—
d the fiddle played on the knee the *viola da gamba*—viola
the knee. Nowadays, the term viola da gamba generally
fers to the 'cello-sized viol.

The two kinds of instruments existed and developed side
side until the early 1700s, when the greater popularity
the violin family led to the almost complete disappearance

of the viols from the musical scene. During their coexistence
the two families of bowed instruments tended to grow more
like each other in shape, each borrowing something from the
other. Often, the same craftsmen made both kinds of in
strument.

The Early Makers

The first violins were made sometime during the 1500s
Violins certainly existed by 1550, when they were used to
entertain the French king Henry III on a visit to Rouen
Despite the claims made on behalf of various makers, it i
impossible to state who the first violin-maker was. A few
violins, violas, 'cellos, and double-basses made in the 1500
still exist, however, and from them we can say that th
earliest makers include Andrea Amati (1505?-1580?)
Gasparo Bertolotti (1540-1609), known as Gasparo de Sal
from the Italian town where he was born, and Giovann
Paolo Maggini (1580-1632?). A claim is sometimes pu
forward for a German, Gaspard Duiffoprugcar (1514?
1570?), who was born in the Tyrol and later lived in Franc
and Italy. It is known that he made viols, but not for certai
whether he built violins.

The great home of violin-making in the 1500s, 1600s, an
1700s was northern Italy, and in particular the towns c
Cremona and Brescia. The climate there is ideal for seasor
ing wood and drying varnish; and Italy at that period cor
tained many great composers, players, and teachers of th
violin. It was also the birthplace of the Renaissance: th
works of Raphael and Leonardo da Vinci were still nev
and Titian and Tintoretto were painting their masterpiece
at about the time the earliest violin-makers were carvin
their instruments and evolving the beautiful shape of th
violin as we know it today. In such an atmosphere, n
wonder the craft of the violin-maker flourished.

Andrea Amati's sons, Antonio and Girolamo (Hierony
mus), carried on their father's trade in the little town c

Cremona in the early 1600s. Girolamo's son, Nicola (1596–1684), was the greatest of the Amati family. He made many fine violins, and trained many violin-makers, among them Antonio Stradivari (1644–1737), who is generally accepted as the greatest of all makers. The earliest violins were made with highly-arched backs and bellies. Stradivari flattened the back and belly and gradually changed the shape of the violin until it was more or less as it is today. Another of Nicola Amati's pupils was Andreas Guarneri (1626–1698), the first of the Guarneri family of makers. The greatest member of this family was Giuseppe Antonio Guarneri (1683–1745), known as Giuseppe del Jesù from the monogram I.H.S. (Iesu Hominum Salvator) with which he always marked his violins. Many of his violins are considered to be as fine as those of Stradivari.

Jacob Stainer (1620?–1683), the greatest of the German makers, may have been another of Nicola Amati's pupils. He certainly worked in Italy for a time. For many years, Stainer's violins were more highly prized than those of Stradivari, because of their sweet tone. Their comparative lack of power eventually caused them to lose favour. A great violin-making industry sprang up in Bavaria, where there was a tradition of fine wood-carving that persists to this day. In places such as Füssen and Mittenwald, near the Austrian frontier, a positive production-line of violin making developed, with individual craftsmen specialising in making one part only of a violin. The result was a host of excellently constructed fiddles, of which the individual parts were well-made, but not necessarily well-matched. By the law of averages, a few superb instruments were produced by accident under this system, along with thousands of lesser instruments. A similar industry later grew up at Mirecourt, near Paris. During the 1700s, a number of good violins were made in Britain. Leading British makers of the period included Benjamin Banks (1727–1795), Richard Duke (1709?–1780), and William Forster (1739–1808).

The Earliest Music

The first music played on violins was ensemble music de
signed to be played on whatever instruments were available
flutes, oboes, recorders, viols, violins, and so on. Often, th
instruments doubled or replaced voice parts in church an
other music. Both viols and violins were named in the scor
of Claudio Monteverdi's opera *Orfeo* (1607). Technical ski
to exploit the possibilities of the superb instruments that th
Amatis, Stradivari, and their contemporaries and successor
were making soon developed in Italy and Germany. Thi
development soon led to the composition of music speciall
for the violin. Among the performer-teacher-composers o
this period were Giovanni Battista Vitali (1644?-1692), an
Archangelo Corelli (1653-1713). Corelli founded the Italia
school, or art, of violin playing, and his influence on th
development of technique was enormous. In the 1700s, a
host of great musicians extended the frontiers of violi
music, and handed on traditions of skill and style from on
generation to the next. As quicker movement of the lef
hand was needed, the position of the violin was raise
so that instead of resting on the arm it was held firml
under the chin. The tradition of players who were also com
posers and teachers continued. Among the most importan
were Antonio Vivaldi (1675?-1741), Francesco Maria
Veracini (1685-1750), Giuseppe Tartini (1692-1770) and Jea
Baptiste Viotti (1753-1824). Viotti is generally regarde
as the principal founder of the modern school of violi
playing.

Many other composers who played the violin but wer
not primarily violinists also wrote music for the instrument
among them Johann Sebastian Bach (1685-1750), Georg
Frideric Handel (1685-1759), and Wolfgang Amadeu
Mozart (1756-1791). Textbooks on violin playing wer
written, two of the most important of the time being by
Francesco Geminiani (1687-1762), and Mozart's father
Leopold Mozart (1719-1787).

The Development of the Bow

Although the violin had reached nearly its final form by the early 1700s, the bow had not. The earliest bows were made of springy wood, curving away from the hair, and with only crude devices for regulating the tension of the hair. Players often held these bows some inches up the stick from the nut. The length was not standard. By the middle of the 1700s, however, a fairly standard type of bow was in general use. It was lighter in attack than the modern bow, and did not lend itself so readily to long, sustained strokes. On the other hand, repeated bow strokes were not so harsh as with a modern bow, and for this reason players of the Bach period tended to use more bow strokes, and not to slur many notes together as later players did, and do. With the old bow, the effect of separate strokes was not so jerky as it can easily be with a modern bow.

In the second half of the 1700s, the bow underwent a revolution comparable to the perfection of the violin under the hand of Stradivari. The man responsible for this revolution was François Tourte (1747–1835), a Parisian. He established the present downward-curving form of the stick, and also discovered that Pernambuco wood was the ideal material for bows. His father, also a bow-maker, had already introduced the screw-operated nut. Tourte's new bow opened up great possibilities for the players. Long bow strokes, greater attack, new forms of bouncing and thrown strokes, were all added to the violinist's repertory. Viotti, who advised Tourte in his perfection of the bow, was one of the first to explore the possibilities of the new bow. If you compare the long runs on single bow strokes and "fancy" bowings in his concertos and those of later composers with the separate bow strokes used so much in the violin works of Corelli, Bach, or Tartini, you will see the revolution the new bow brought to violin music.

Later Developments

The new style of music brought about the final change in the form of the violin. The increased virtuosity of performers demanded a more brilliant tone, greater power, and greater freedom for fingering. These were achieved by raising the pitch slightly, increasing the height of the bridge, and lengthening the strings. To accommodate the higher bridge, the neck had to be set at an angle to the instrument's body, instead of being parallel with it as before. The neck also had to be lengthened to allow for the increased length of the strings. Because the longer strings and higher pitch increased the pressure of the strings on the belly, a heavier bass-bar was fitted inside the violin to support it. All new instruments were made to the new pattern, and most older instruments were gradually altered. The change suited the flat-arched Stradivari violins, but did not suit so well the higher-arched instruments such as those of Stainer or Amati. As a result, Stainer's violins declined in popularity.

During the 1800s, two French violin-makers came to the fore, Nicholas Lupot (1758–1824), and Jean-Baptiste Vuillaume (1798–1875). Vuillaume was one of the greatest violin craftsmen who has ever lived, and he made superb copies of the work of the great Italian violin-makers, particularly Stradivari. During this period, too, the desire for Italian violins was fostered, and fulfilled, by an Italian repairer and dealer, Luigi Tarisio. Tarisio wandered all over Italy, buying old instruments from peasants who were often glad to exchange a broken old Stradivari, Amati, Bergonzi, or other now-famous make for a shiny new fiddle in perfect order. Tarisio sold these great master instruments in Paris, most of them to Vuillaume. Tarisio's work in collecting and preserving so many of the great violins of the Italian masters is of unique importance in the history of the instrument.

On the playing side, skill and teaching continued to make progress. The outstanding figure was Niccolò Paganini (1782–1840), whose fantastic technique was for a time the amazement of concert-goers all over Europe. Other great names of the century include Pierre Rode (1774–1830), Rodolphe Kreutzer (1766–1831), Ludwig Spohr (1784–1859), Joseph Joachim (1831–1904), and Eugène Ysaÿe (1858–1931). In the early years of the twentieth century, Fritz Kreisler (1875–1963) led the way in the use of a continuous vibrato on every sustained note.

The history of the violin is not yet over. Music by modern composers has demanded further changes of technique. Research into the construction of violins is being carried out in America and Europe. New materials have been tested and used for strings. Many kinds of shoulder-rests have been developed. Modern bow-makers, too, are keeping up with progress. They have great need to, for, unlike violins, bows can wear out comparatively quickly from over-much use. The spread of radio and good recorded music has enabled more young students to study the work and techniques of the great players of the day, and has helped to raise the overall standard of performance to even higher levels.

18. Minor Repairs

Whenever possible, all repair work, particularly on a valuable instrument, should be entrusted to an expert. For major repairs it is worth while travelling a distance to make sure that you entrust them to a violin-maker, and not just to "the man who does fiddles" at the local piano shop. The man who does fiddles may be, and sometimes is, an expert. But often he is not. Try to find out about him from other local violinists.

There are, however, some minor repairs which the amateur can tackle himself, if he is careful. A knowledge of how to do them can be most useful, especially if something goes wrong at a time when it is not possible to get the violin to a skilled repairer.

The Pegs

A slipping peg is a common nuisance. If the peg appears to be fitting properly, you can try rubbing it with soap, and then dusting it with French chalk. Alternatively, rub the peg on the underside of the bow-hair, so that it picks up a little rosin. Check also that you have wound the string on correctly as described in Chapter 4.

If neither of these methods works, the peg is probably not fitting correctly in the holes in the peg-box. Do not touch the holes in any circumstances: you can easily do severe damage to the instrument, which will then require an expensive, expert repair to put right. Instead, remove the peg and look at it carefully. There should be two shiny bands round it where it engages in the peg-box. If these bands do not extend right round, then the peg is not fitting properly.

With a sharp knife, a razor-blade, or a small piece of newly-broken glass, scrape the smallest possible amount off the peg where the shine shows, which is where the high spots are. Turn the peg in the holes again to put the shine back on. The area of shiny peg should have increased. Repeat the treatment until the shiny bands extend right round the peg. The peg is now fitting properly. If the peg is badly worn, or if there are cracks in the peg-box near the holes, you will need new pegs or repairs to the peg-box. Fitting a complete new set of pegs or mending cracks of this kind are tasks that must be left to a violin-maker.

Replacing Tail-Gut

Another job that occasionally needs doing is replacing the tail-gut. Buy a few inches of tail-gut from your music-shop or violin dealer. Push the two ends through the holes in the tail-piece, so that a loop is left at the end of the tail-piece. Hold one end of the tail-gut in the flame of a match or a candle until it sizzles and swells up. Tie thread tightly round the end. This makes a knob that is large enough not to pull through the hole in the tail-piece. Now try the tail-piece in position, and leave a loop big enough for the tail-piece just to clear the little ebony saddle at the end of the violin. Mark the position, remove the tail-piece, cut the surplus off the other end of the tail-gut, and treat that end with flame and thread to make a second knob. The job is then complete. If the tail-gut snaps at an awkward time when you cannot get a fresh piece, a temporary repair can be made with any thick piece of gut, such as a piece of a 'cello string. If no gut is available, a length of wire will do until you can effect a proper repair. String or cord will not serve, because it will stretch too much.

The Bridge

You should check your bridge from time to time. Make sure that it is in the right place, with both feet firmly on

the violin-belly, leaning slightly towards the tail-piece. I
should not bend, but sometimes bridges do bend on the I
string side. If your bridge is bent, slacken the strings
enough so that you can coax it straight with the fingers, and
then bring the strings back to pitch. Straighten a bridge
carefully and gently. It is easy to break a bridge, and
fitting a new one is a task for an expert. The usual cause
of bending is a string binding in its notch instead of slipping
easily over it. You should lubricate the notch by rubbing i
with a pencil as described in Chapter 4.

Cleaning

To clean a violin is a straightforward task. The regular
wiping over that you do after playing should keep the out
side clean. If further cleaning is needed, use a small amount
of good quality furniture cream (not wax or silicone pol
ishes). This cream will remove most dried rosin. Dust inside
instruments can sometimes be removed with the aid of the
dusting tools of a vacuum-cleaner. Apply the nozzle of a
suitable tool to one f-hole, covering the other f-hole with a
piece of paper to help create suction. Be careful not to press
or scratch the surface of the instrument while applying the
tools to the f-holes, and do not attempt to pass anything
through the f-holes. More elaborate cleaning is best done by
an expert.

Glueing Up Back and Belly

In damp weather, the back or the belly sometimes become
unglued from the ribs for an inch or so. A violin-maker re
pairs this fault by running a little hot glue into the gap, and
clamping it until the glue has set. You can tackle this repair
quite easily. You need some ordinary scotch glue, of the kind
that is heated in a glue-kettle. Do *not* under any circum
stances use any of the modern acetate or impact adhesives
or you will ruin the fiddle. With glue, the instrument can b
opened for repairs should these become necessary in th

future. With a more powerful adhesive, it cannot. You can, however, use any proprietary glue that can be softened by heat.

Take a worn table knife and insert it very carefully in the gap to open the crack slightly. Clean out the old glue with a small brush slightly moistened with hot water. Be careful not to extend the gap. Warm the glue, and put a little into the gap with the tip of the knife. Use as little glue as possible, and use it thin, diluting it with hot water if necessary. The joint must now be clamped. There is one ready-made clamp always available for this sort of repair. Take the chin-rest away from its accustomed place on the lower bouts, and tighten it cautiously over the place where you are gluing. Wipe any surplus glue away at once with hot water and a rag. Be careful not to let the water into the interior of the instrument, and dry the surface with a soft cloth.

If you want to make a clamp for such repairs, that is also quite easy. You need a 2½-in. or 3-in. coach bolt with a wing-nut. Make two collars of wood about half an inch thick, to slip easily on the bolt. A cotton-reel cut in half with the holes enlarged would make a suitable collar. You use the bolt with a collar each side of the violin as a clamp. Beware of tightening the clamp too much: the lightest pressure will be enough, and more might break the back, belly, or ribs. In all gluing jobs, leave the glue to set for twenty-four hours, or at least overnight.

The symptoms of unglued back or belly are often a rattle or a loss of power from the instrument. To detect the loose part, tap carefully all round the edge of the back and belly with a finger-knuckle. The loose part will rattle when struck. Usually, however, you will see the gap where the back or belly is springing away from the ribs.

Buzzes and Wolf-Notes

As we have seen, a buzz may be caused if the violin is coming unglued. But the most common cause of buzzing is a loose covering on a covered string. This covering consists of fine wire wound on a gut core. If the gut core becomes hard with age and shrinks, the wire will rattle against it. There is no satisfactory cure except to replace the string. If the core has shrunk, the string is probably coming to the end of its useful life anyway. Some violin repairers used to advocate soaking the string in almond oil to swell up the gut, wiping the string carefully afterwards. To detect a buzzing string, play several notes on it. If there are buzzes on all of them, and none on other strings, the string is defective.

Other causes of buzzes are a loose string-adjuster, or part of the knot of a string catching on the belly of the violin under the tail-piece. Loose gold mounts in the ends of pegs and tail-pins can also buzz. The cures are obvious: string ends should be trimmed so that they are clear of the belly, and a drop of glue will secure a loose mount.

A wolf-note is an extraneous note that sounds when certain notes are played. It may be caused by the back or the belly coming loose. Generally, however, the cause is more radical, and needs expert attention to put it right. Occasionally unevenness in the finger-board can cause unwanted noises. The cure is to plane the finger-board true again, but this is also a job for the expert.

The golden rule in all repairs is: if in doubt, leave it to a violin-maker to put the trouble right. Those who want to learn more about the construction and repair of violins are recommended to read *Violin-Making: As It Was and Is*, by Ed. Heron-Allen (Ward Lock). This book, first published in 1884, is a classic work on the subject, and is still kept in print.

19. The Viola

The viola is the tenor instrument of the violin family, its strings sounding a fifth lower than those of the violin. The cello is the bass of the family, soprano and alto parts being taken as a rule by violins. The viola is similar in construction and shape to a violin, and is held under the chin and played in the same manner. It is larger than a violin, but not so large in proportion to the pitch of its deepest note. This undersized element gives viola tone a more mournful, haunting sound than the tone of a violin or 'cello. This tone is an essential part of string quartets and the string section of orchestras. As a result of neglect for many years, there is less music for the viola than for either the violin or the cello. However, modern composers are making up for previous indifference, and skilful arrangements of music written for other instruments are also now available.

The Choice of a Viola

The kind of viola you choose depends on the purpose for which you wish to use it. The size of violas, unlike that of violins and 'cellos, has never been standardised, makers facing a constant compromise between tone—which demands a large instrument—and ease of playing—which demands a small one. The body length of violas, measured from the root of the button below the neck down the back, ranges from 15 inches to 18 inches, and examples larger and smaller than this also exist. If you plan to play the viola as an alternative to the violin, you should choose one with a body length of about 15½ inches or 16 inches. An instrument smaller than 15½ inches is not likely to have a sufficiently good tone for normal quartet or orchestral work. A larger viola may present fingering problems. The difference in stretch between the violin and a 15½-inch viola is not great, and the hand can adapt easily to it without encountering intonation difficulties on either instrument. The greater stretch of a large instrument makes changing from one to another at will a more hazardous occupation. If you plan to play the viola as your main instrument, using the violin only on rare occasions, then choose a bigger instrument by all means. Bear in mind that the length of your arms and fingers will affect your choice. A person with small hands and short arms will have difficulty with the larger sizes of viola.

As for the actual instrument, the same considerations apply as in choosing a violin. One good test, however, is to play the C-string, the lowest string of the viola. If it sounds like a blow-fly on a window-pane trying to get out, you would be well advised to reject the instrument. It is important to have a proper viola bow. Because the strings are thicker, they need more bow-weight to make them speak freely. Extra pressure applied to the bow will not take the place of extra weight.

The Notes and the Clef

The viola is tuned a fifth below the violin, that is, the four strings are A, D, G, and C. The three upper strings correspond to the three lower strings of the violin. To reduce as far as possible the number of ledger lines used in writing out viola music, it is always written in the alto clef, one of the three C clefs. In this clef, middle C, which is the line below the stave of the treble clef, is the middle line of the clef.

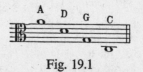

Fig. 19.1

It is easy to learn the alto clef. Remember that the first
and third fingers still play notes on the lines in the first
position, and the second and fourth fingers still play notes
in the spaces.

Higher passages on the viola are written in the treble clef.
They mostly involve playing in the higher positions on the
A-string, but should present no difficulties to a violin player.

Differences in Fingering

Basically, the fingering of the viola is identical with that of
the violin. The fingers are fractionally farther apart, and extensions require a quite noticeable stretch. For this reason,
viola players make a greater use of half-position shifts, often
playing two consecutive notes with the same finger in order
to move up or down the finger-board and have the next
group of notes lying under the fingers. Because of the special
tone-qualities of the instrument, the higher positions on
the lower strings are used much less than on the violin.
The A-string has a brilliant quality that encourages players
to make a greater use of it. Viola players also use open
strings whenever possible, because their increased resonance
does a great deal to brighten the tone of the instrument.

There is one phenomenon peculiar to the viola. If the
open A-string is played at speed between two stopped notes,
it will sound the octave higher. Viola players sometimes
take advantage of this characteristic in playing certain quick
passages. The phenomenon does not occur when playing
slowly.

Differences in Bowing

The viola needs a more resolute style of bowing than the
violin, and its technique in that respect is more akin to that
of the 'cello. It is a mistake to play a viola with a light,
delicate touch; the instrument will not respond, and all you
will get is a rather feeble tone. But bold, sweeping strokes

will bring out to the full its beauties of tone. Strokes such a
a light staccato require a heavier touch than correspondin
strokes on the violin.

History of the Viola

The early history of the viola is parallel to that of the violin
except that some authorities believe that the first true mem
bers of the violin family to be made may have been viola
rather than violins. From the first, the main problem fo
players and makers alike was that of size. Before about 1660
most violas were large—some as big as $18\frac{1}{2}$ inches. Stradi
vari made two sizes of viola to play different parts. Late
violas were mostly about $16\frac{1}{2}$ inches or smaller. Until th
late 1700s composers treated the viola as the Cinderella o
instruments. They wrote dull, simple parts for it, and as
result the standard of viola playing also declined. Violinist
with poor technique took to the viola as a safe refuge wher
their lack of skill would not be noticed. This produced
vicious circle, with composers reluctant to trust viola player
with anything complicated to play. From the time of Haydn
however, the position improved, and composers such a
Mozart (who played the instrument himself) wrote mor
interesting parts for the viola in chamber music.

In the 1800s the situation improved further. Composers o
orchestral and chamber music demanded greater techniqu
from violists—greater than they found, to judge from som
of the things they wrote and said—and teachers and maker
alike began to devote attention to the instrument and it
technique and problems. The emergence of the viola as
solo instrument did not come until the 1900s, when a num
ber of brilliant players, notably Lionel Tertis, demon
strated its possibilities in ways that could not be overlooked
Many composers wrote concertos and other solo pieces fo
Tertis and the other great viola players who followed hin
and Paul Hindemith, himself a fine violist, did much t
extend the repertoire of the instrument. Much other musi

has been transcribed for the viola, some of it not always
successfully. Among music so transcribed are a number of
classical violin sonatas, such as those of Handel, and
classical works for the viola da gamba and wind instruments—the horn, for example. Brilliant yet majestic works,
such as the Vitali Chaconne, are the ones that transcribe
best. A number of 'cello pieces, including the solo suites by
J. S. Bach, have also been added to the viola's repertory.

Glossary of Terms in Violin Music

This glossary contains the most important terms used in connection with violins and string playing, in French, German, and Italian. Most musical instructions are written in Italian, which is regarded as an international language in music. But many composers use French or German, and a few use English. Self-explanatory English terms, and terms dealt with fully elsewhere in this book, are not included. The languages are abbreviated as Fr. (French), Ger. (German), It. (Italian), and Lat. (Latin).

Accelerando, accel. (It.)—Increase the speed.

Absetzen (Ger.)—Staccato, detached.

Abstrich (Ger.)—Down-bow.

Adagio (It.)—Slow.

Ad libitum, ad lib. (Lat.)—At will; generally applied to a solo passage in which the player can vary the time.

Affetuoso (It.)—With tender feeling.

Agitato (It.)—Agitated, restless.

Aria (It.)—An air; usually a singing type of solo.

Al (It.)—Up to, as in *al fine,* to the word *fine* (end).

Alla (It.)—In the manner of; *alla breve,* an indication to regard a minim, not a crochet, as the time unit.

Allargando (It.)—Becoming broader and slower.

Allegretto (It.)—Moderately fast.

Allegro (It.)—Fast; *allegro assai*, very fast; *allegro molto,* very fast; *allegro ma non troppo,* not too fast.

Alle Saiten (Ger.)—On all strings.

Allongé (Fr.)—Prolonged; *allonger l'archet,* to prolong the bow-stroke.

Alto (It.)—The viola; *alto clef*, the C clef used in viola music, with middle C as the middle line of the stave.

Amoroso (It.)—Lovingly, sweetly.

Andante (It.)—Slow, graceful (but generally not extremely slow); *più andante, andantino*, a little faster than andante.

Animato (It.)—In a lively manner.

Appassionato (It.)—With feeling.

Archet (Fr.)—The bow.

Arco (It.)—The bow, with the bow.

Armonici, arm. (It.)—Harmonics.

Arpeggio (It.)—In the style of a harp: the notes are played consecutively and not as a chord.

Assai (It.)—Sufficiently, very; *allegro assai*, very fast.

Attacca (It.)—Go on at once, without a pause.

Aufstrich (Ger.)—Up-bow.

Band (Ger.)—A volume or book.

Ben, Bene (It.)—Well; *ben marcato*, well-marked.

Bogen (Ger.)—The bow, with the bow; *bogenstrich*, bow-stroke.

Braccio (It.)—The arm; *viola da braccio*, a violin or viola.

Bratsche (Ger.)—The viola.

Breve—A note twice the length of a semibreve, now seldom found. It is written

Brio (It.)—Fire; *con brio*, with fire; *brioso*, in a fiery manner.

Cadenza (It.)—A portion of a concerto played by the soloist unaccompanied, originally improvised.

Calando (It.)—Decreasing in sound.

Cantabile (It.)—In a singing style; also *cantando*.

Capo (It.)—Beginning; *da capo*, from the beginning.

Cedez (Fr.)—Decrease the tone.

Coda (It.)—An extra concluding section.

Col, coll', colla (It.)—With; *col arco*, with the bow; *colla parte*, with the soloist.

Come (It.)—As, exactly; *come primo*, as at first.

Comodo, commodo (It.)—Without haste.

Con (It.)—With; as in *con brio*, with fire.

Corda (It.)—A string; *corde*, strings; *a una corda*, on one string; *a due corde*, on two strings.

Crescendo, cres. (It.)—Increase the tone.

Da Capo, D.C. (It.)—Repeat from the beginning; *da capo senza replica*, from the beginning without other repeats.

Dal Segno (It.)—Repeat from the sign (2).

Decrescendo, decres. (It.)—Decrease the tone.

Détaché (Fr.)—Detached or staccato notes.

Diminuendo, dim. (It.)—Decreasing.

Divisi (It.)—Divided, indicating that one of a pair of instruments plays the upper line, and the other the lower line.

Dolce (It.)—Sweetly.

Doppelgriff (Ger.)—A double-stop.

Dur (Ger.)—Major; *G dur*, G major.

Fine (It.)—End; indicates the end of a repeated section.

Flageolet (Fr.)—Harmonic.

Forte, f (It.)—Loud; *fortissimo*, (*ff*, *fff*, *ffff*), very loudly.

Forza (It.)—Emphasis; *con forza*, with emphasis.

Ganz (Ger.)—Whole; *ganzer bogen, G.B.,* whole-bow.

Geige (Ger.)—Violin; *geiger*, violinist.

Glissando (It.)—Sliding.

Glissez (Fr.)—Glide, slide.

Grave (It.)— Slow or solemn.

Grazioso (It.)—Gracefully.

H. (Ger.)—The note B; *B* (Ger.), the note B♭.

Herunterstrich (Ger.)—Down-bow.

Hinaufstrich (Ger.)—Up-bow.

Hinstrich (Ger.)—Up-bow.

Inhalt (Ger.)—Table of contents.

Istesso Tempo (It.)—The same tempo.

Jetez (Fr.)—Throw, as in a thrown-bow stroke.

Lage (Ger.)—Position; *erste lage,* first position; *lagen-weschel,* change of position.

Langsamer (Ger.)—Slower.

Largamente (It.)—Broadly, grandly.

Largo (It.)—Slow, broad; *larghetto,* moderately slow.

Lebhaft (Ger.)—Lively, quick.

Legato (It.)—Smooth, connected, not staccato; generally a flowing style of bowing.

Léger (Fr.)—Light; *légèrement,* lightly.

Leggiero (It.)—Light, easy; *leggieramente,* lightly, swiftly; *leggierezza,* with lightness; *leggierissimo,* very light.

Legno (It.)—Wood; *coll' legno,* with the back of the bow.

Leicht (Ger.)—Lightly.

Leise (Ger.)—Low, soft.

Lento (It.)—Slow.

Libitus (Lat.)—Pleasure; *ad libitum,* at will.

Loco (It.)—Play in place, as written; used after passages marked *8va,* meaning play an octave higher.

Lunga (It.)—Long; *lunga pausa,* a long pause.

Ma (It.)—But; *ma non troppo,* but not too much.

Maestoso (It.)—Majestic, dignified.

Maggiore (It.)—Major, in a major key.

Marcato, marc. (It.)—Marked or emphasised.

Massig (Ger.)—Moderately.

Mehr (Ger.)—More.

Meno (It.)—Less; *meno mosso,* less fast.

Mezza, Mezzo (It.)—Half, medium; *mezzo forte (mf),* moderately loud; *mezzo piano (mp),* moderately soft.

Minore (It.)—Minor, in a minor key.

Mit (Ger.)—With.

Moderato (It.)—Moderate.

Moll (Ger.)—Minor; *G moll,* G minor.

Molto (It.)—Much, very; *molto vivace,* very lively.

Morendo (It.)—Dying away.

Mosso (It.)—Rapid, moved; *meno mosso,* less rapid.

Moto (It.)—Movement, motion; *con moto,* with movement.

Noch (Ger.)—Still more; *noch schneller,* still quicker.

Non (It.)—Not; *allegro non troppo*, not too fast.

Obbligato (It.)—Usually an independent melody, accompanying a song or other solo part.

Opus, Op. (It.)—Work.

Ossia (It.)—Alternative, usually an easier substitute for a difficult passage.

Ottava, 8va (It.)—An octave higher, the direction continuing in force to the limit of a dotted line over the notes.

Perdendosi (It.)—Dying away in speed and sound.

Pesante (It.)—Ponderous, heavy.

Piano, p (It.)—Soft, gentle; *pianissimo* (*pp, ppp, pppp*), as quietly as possible.

Più (It.)—More; *più vivace*, more lively.

Pizzicato, pizz. (It.)—Plucked with the fingers; *pizz. l.h.*, pluck with the fingers of the left hand.

Poco (It.)—A little; *poco a poco*, little by little.

Ponticello (It.)—The bridge; *sul ponticello*, near the bridge.

Portamento (It.)—Gliding, a bowed glissando.

Poussé (Fr.)—Up-bow.

Presto (It.)—Quick; *prestissimo*, very quick.

Prima, primo (It.)—First; *prima volta*, first time.

Principale (It.)—Principal; *violino principale*, solo violin.

Principalstimme (Ger.)—Solo part.

Quasi (It.)—Almost; *quasi allegro*, almost quickly.

Quitter (Fr.)—To leave; *sans quitter la corde*, without leaving the string.

Rallentando, rall. (It.)—Gradually slower.

Répétez (Fr.)—Repeat.

Replica (It.)—Repeat.

Restez (Fr.)—Remain; usually in the sense of *restez à la position*, remain in the same position.

Risoluto (It.)—With resolution.

Ritard, rit. (It.)—Slower; also *ritardando*.

Ritenuto (It.)—Holding back the speed.

Rubato (It.)—Usually short for *tempo rubato*, in which one note is robbed of part of its value so as to lengthen another.

Saite (Ger.)—String.

Sattel (Ger.)—The nut of the finger-board.

Scharf (Ger.)—Sharp, acute; *scharf abgestossen*, broad staccato.

Scherzo (It.)—Joke; *scherzando, scherzoso*, jestingly.

Schnell (Ger.)—Quick; *schneller*, quicker.

Schwach (Ger.)—Weak, soft.

Schwer (Ger.)—Difficult; *mittelschwer*, moderately hard.

Segno (It.)—Sign; *dal segno*, from the sign.

Segue (It.)—Play in the same manner.

Sehr (Ger.)—Very.

Semper, semp. (Lat.)—Always.

Semplice (It.)—Simply.

Senza (It.)—Without; *senza sordino*, without a mute.

Sforzando, sf. (It.)—With force or emphasis.

Simile, Simili (It.)—Like.

Smorzando (It.)—Gradually fading away.

Sonore (Fr.)—Sonorous, resonant.

Sordino (It.)—Mute; *con sordino*, with the mute; *senza sordino,* without the mute; *sourdine* (Fr.)—Mute.

Spitz (Ger.)—The point of the bow.

Staccato (It.)—Detached, each note separated sharply.

Stark (Ger.)—Vigorous, strong.

Steg (Ger.)—Bridge; *am steg*, at the bridge.

Streich (Ger.)—Bow-stroke; *streichen,* to bow.

Stringendo (It.)—Hastening the time.

Stück (Ger.)—A piece.

Subito (It.)—Immediately; *volti subito, v.s.,* turn over at once.

Suivez (Fr.)—Follow.

Sul (It.)—On, near; *sul ponticello*, near the bridge; *sul tasto*, near the finger-board.

Sur (Fr.)—On, over; *sur la touche*, over the finger-board.

Tacet (Lat.)—Be silent.

Talon (Fr.)—Heel (of the bow).

Tanto (It.)—So much.

Tempo (It.)—Time; *a tempo*, back to time.

Tenuto, ten. (It.)—Hold for full value.

Tirez (Fr.)—Down-bow.

Ton (Fr.)—Tone, pitch.

Touche (Fr.)—Finger-board.

Tout (Fr.)—All; *tout l'archet*, whole-bow.

Tremolo (It.)—Trembling; played with a rapid movement of the right wrist.

Tutta Forza (It.)—Full force.

Tutti (It.)—All; generally indicates that the whole band plays.

Und (Ger.)—And.

Vivace, viv. (It.)—Lively; *vivacissimo,* very lively.

Vivo (It.)—Lively; *vivamente*, in a lively manner.

Volante (It.)—In a light, flying manner.

Volta (It.)—Time; *prima volta*, first time; *secunda volta*, second time.

Volti Subito, V.S. (It.)—Turn over quickly.

Wenig (Ger.)—Little.

Wie (Ger.)—As.

Zart (Ger.)—Soft.

Zeit (Ger.)—Time.

Index

Index

For musical terms, see the Glossary. Some musical terms which are extensively treated in the text are also listed here.